Other Winter Goose titles
by Ina Schroders-Zeeders

> *Veritas*
>
> *Amor*
>
> *Roads Book1*

# ROADS
## BOOK 2

**INA SCHRODERS-ZEEDERS**

This publication is a creative work protected in full by all applicable copyright laws, as well as by misappropriation, trade secret, unfair competition, and other applicable laws. No part of this book may be reproduced or transmitted in any manner without written permission from Winter Goose Publishing, except in the case of brief quotations embodied in critical articles or reviews. All rights reserved.

Winter Goose Publishing
45 Lafayette Road #114
North Hampton, NH 03862

www.wintergoosepublishing.com
Contact Information: info@wintergoosepublishing.com

Roads Book 2

COPYRIGHT © 2016 by Ina Schroders-Zeeders

First Edition, April 2016

Cover Design by Winter Goose Publishing
Cover Art Picture by David Agnew
Typesetting by Odyssey Books

ISBN: 978-1-941058-38-1

Published in the United States of America

*To my granddaughters*

*Eline and Ronja*

# Contents

| | |
|---|---:|
| **I The Never Ending Road** | 1 |
| Back Home | 3 |
| Intensions | 4 |
| City | 5 |
| The Secret | 6 |
| Wisdom | 8 |
| Time | 9 |
| Winter Idyll | 10 |
| Bloody Christmas | 11 |
| The Moment | 12 |
| Heathen in Church | 13 |
| The Pretender | 14 |
| A Caring Woman in Winter | 15 |
| Writer | 16 |
| Sunday Surprise in the Seventies | 17 |
| Garden Tea Party | 19 |
| Waiting in the Hospital | 20 |
| I Met Rumi on the Ferry | 21 |
| Deep Thought on the Ferry | 22 |
| Rather Knackered | 23 |
| Inspection Day | 24 |
| The Old Chair | 27 |
| Going Vertigo | 28 |
| Confession of a Would Be Sinner | 29 |
| The Last Assembling | 30 |
| Nightingales | 32 |
| The Thought Collector | 33 |
| My Life Compares Itself to a Hangover | 35 |
| Darkness | 37 |

| | |
|---|---|
| Her Husband Is in Hospital | 38 |
| Miracle | 39 |
| Observation | 40 |
| Clean | 41 |
| Listening | 42 |
| P | 43 |
| Aftertaste | 44 |
| Nights with Minds of Their Own | 45 |
| For | 47 |
| Passion Fever | 48 |
| On Hot Days | 50 |
| Ha! | 51 |
| Word to Ponder | 52 |
| Create! | 53 |
| Losing It | 54 |
| Extraction | 55 |
| Harbour Men | 56 |
| Sunny Day | 57 |
| The Cycle of Life | 58 |
| The Taste of Fruit | 59 |
| When We Were Three and Four | 60 |
| Summer Heat | 61 |
| To Be Two Cats | 62 |
| Doing Dishes | 63 |
| Chaos | 64 |
| Child's Play | 65 |
| The First Mate's Daughter | 66 |
| The Landing | 67 |
| The Town with Many Statues | 68 |
| Yet | 69 |
| Almost Forgot | 70 |
| Village | 71 |
| March of Horror | 72 |

| | |
|---|---:|
| Secret Lives on Bus Rides | 73 |
| Poems About Love | 74 |
| Birds of a Feather 1 | 75 |
| Crisis Conference | 76 |
| Foreign Esses | 77 |
| As the Moon Does | 79 |
| Souvenirs de Gravelines | 80 |
| Not with the Program | 82 |
| White | 83 |
| Horizon Birds | 84 |
| Grave Stone | 85 |
| Verbal | 86 |
| Under Skies at Night | 87 |
| Yet to Read | 88 |
| Invited for Tea | 89 |
| Nights | 91 |
| Moon | 92 |
| To Love | 93 |
| Home | 94 |
| Cortege | 95 |
| His Brother Wore Lederhosen | 96 |
| Welcome to the Island | 97 |
| So Tired Is This World | 98 |
| Christmas Stable | 99 |
| Christmas Spirit | 100 |
| Time 1 | 101 |
| The Ferry Fly | 102 |
| Hibernatory Mood | 103 |
| Scent of a Wanted Space | 104 |
| Heirs to the Bone | 105 |
| Old Woman | 106 |
| From the Land of Cuthim | 108 |
| Poultry | 109 |

| | |
|---|---|
| Standing by the Stone | 110 |
| Space | 111 |
| Timing | 112 |
| Poems Among Poems | 113 |
| The Moment We Made Gods | 114 |
| This Borrowed Life | 115 |
| Not Yet | 116 |
| The Café Lieman | 117 |
| Walking to the End in Rain and Hail | 118 |
| Frame Rate 25 | 119 |
| Rain on Graveyards | 120 |
| The Sake of Art | 121 |
| Nature Wise | 122 |
| Rape Seed | 123 |
| In Thoughts We Live | 125 |
| Bone China | 126 |
| Meeting Again | 127 |
| Early Morning Thought | 128 |
| Basic Weather Poem | 129 |
| Flummoxed | 130 |
| Bloody Mess | 131 |
| Why 1 | 132 |
| The Sound | 133 |
| Be Like a Butterfly | 134 |
| Goodbye (for N) | 135 |
| Night in the Attic | 136 |
| Logic | 138 |
| Landscape After War | 139 |
| Survival of the Fittest Heart | 140 |
| What is Time | 141 |
| To Being Fly | 142 |
| Tree | 143 |
| The Origin of Mermaids | 144 |

| | |
|---|---:|
| Where Warmth Now Lies | 145 |
| Waiting for the Right Time We Die | 146 |
| Droste Tin | 147 |
| Heroes | 148 |
| Comfort in Times of Grief | 149 |
| Forget Me, Nut | 150 |
| Ghost | 151 |
| Night Delivery | 152 |
| Nomads in Pain | 153 |
| Islanders | 154 |
| Dream House | 155 |
| Meaning? | 157 |
| Today | 158 |
| Our Story | 159 |
| It | 160 |
| The Deal | 161 |
| The Arriving of the Omen | 162 |
| This Change | 163 |
| Ninety Something | 164 |
| Evening Shades | 165 |
| It Is the Way It Is | 166 |
| Images | 167 |
| Words | 168 |
| Marrakech | 169 |
| Children in a Graveyard | 170 |
| The Crow 1 | 171 |
| What Lies Beneath | 172 |
| Nehalennia | 173 |
| Grave Days | 174 |
| Leningrad | 175 |
| The Poem | 177 |
| Pin Up | 178 |
| Why 2 | 179 |

| | |
|---|---|
| To Choose a Dream | 180 |
| Lake View | 181 |
| Diving Up | 182 |
| Morning in April, 2014 | 183 |
| Despair | 184 |
| This is an Island | 185 |
| Why Winter Weeps | 186 |
| Deceit | 187 |
| Finding Truth | 188 |
| Be a Dreamer | 189 |
| | |
| **II The Road to England** | 191 |
| The Cliff | 193 |
| Behind the Cliff | 194 |
| The Stone | 195 |
| Fish | 196 |
| Whitby Museum Artefact | 197 |
| Downton Abbey | 198 |
| The City | 200 |
| In Henrietta Street Now it is Noon | 201 |
| At Six P.M. Somewhere in March | 202 |
| These Men Have Been Here Forever | 203 |
| There Must Be Ways | 204 |
| Almost There | 205 |
| Yorkshire Wise | 206 |
| Whitby | 208 |
| Segedunum | 210 |
| Driftwood | 211 |
| | |
| **III The Road Through Nature** | 213 |
| Storm | 215 |
| Abhorrence | 216 |
| Instinct by Nature | 217 |

| | |
|---|---|
| Trees and Old People | 218 |
| Swan | 219 |
| The Tree That Said Farewell | 220 |
| Geese Flight | 221 |
| Autumn (In Three Languages) | 223 |
| Automne | 224 |
| Herfst | 225 |
| The Alien | 226 |
| Autumn Gala | 227 |
| Amazed | 228 |
| Blue Forever | 229 |
| Dance Trees | 230 |
| The Mother Buzzard | 231 |
| Motherhood | 232 |
| Late Spring | 233 |
| Frosted Air | 234 |
| The Feelings of Flowers | 235 |
| Swans Know | 236 |
| Grey Sunday in February | 237 |
| I Take the End of Winter Bad | 238 |
| Return | 239 |
| Frosted Still | 240 |
| See This Tree | 241 |
| The Crow 2 | 242 |
| 10 Beaufort | 243 |
| Just a Bit of May | 244 |
| Where It Was | 245 |
| The Trees | 247 |
| Past Trees | 248 |
| Indigo Night | 249 |
| Under the Ice | 251 |
| Birds of a Feather 2 | 252 |
| The Poetry of Birds | 253 |

| | |
|---|---|
| January Laziness | 254 |
| Anti-climax at Eleven | 255 |
| Their Branches Curving | 256 |
| Morning Flirt | 257 |
| | |
| **IV The Road to the Family Tree** | 259 |
| Watching from the Past | 261 |
| Connection | 262 |
| Grandfather 1 | 263 |
| Becoming Mother | 264 |
| Cold Start | 265 |
| Tall He Stood There | 266 |
| Family | 267 |
| Warmth | 268 |
| Nose | 269 |
| Father's Hand | 270 |
| Father 1 | 271 |
| Grandfather 2 | 274 |
| The Blossom | 275 |
| Time 2 | 276 |
| Like | 277 |
| So Like You | 278 |
| The Man Becomes My Father | 279 |
| Old Ships in Mist | 280 |
| Son | 281 |
| Caught | 282 |
| The Child is Here | 283 |
| Last Time | 284 |
| Old Man of Mine | 285 |
| Togetherness | 286 |
| Mothers | 288 |
| I Would Not Fit in My Own Childhood as a Mother | 290 |
| Mensch | 291 |

| | |
|---|---:|
| Aunt | 293 |
| Father 2 | 294 |
| Floating Marigolds | 295 |
| Kitschy Moments | 296 |
| Aware | 297 |
| Your Face, Your Voice | 300 |
| Needed | 301 |
| Older | 302 |
| The Call | 303 |
| Teaching Eline How to Walk | 304 |
| Never Be Before | 305 |
| Chain | 306 |
| Shadows | 307 |
| Why Mothers Cry | 308 |
| On the Bus | 309 |
| Rejection | 310 |
| Generations | 312 |
| | |
| **V The Road to the Sea** | **313** |
| The Sea Is My Mother | 315 |
| Mist | 316 |
| Forgotten Vision | 317 |
| The Place | 318 |
| My View | 319 |
| Sea Dance | 320 |
| The Book | 321 |
| The Tide Turning | 322 |
| Standing on a Dune | 323 |
| Grain | 324 |
| On the Beach | 325 |
| Shadow | 326 |
| Worth the Walk | 327 |
| Possibilities | 328 |

| | |
|---|---|
| Rain on a Dune | 329 |
| Waiting for the Tide to Kill Me | 330 |
| Homesick of the Sea | 331 |
| Murmuration | 332 |
| Wrecked | 333 |
| The Last Thing | 334 |
| Ambergris | 335 |
| Sea | 336 |
| Lost | 337 |
| Alone I Walk | 338 |
| Moment of Silence | 339 |
| Misty Morning in November | 340 |
| Best of Mornings | 341 |
| Best of Gifts | 342 |
| Learning to Live | 343 |
| Devastated | 344 |
| Washed Ashore | 345 |
| Acknowledgments | 347 |
| About the Author | 348 |

# I
## The Never Ending Road

# Back Home

The journey is over. The suitcases, unpacked,
are collecting dust again in the attic.
We know more now, we saw and learned.

But here at home, the house has changed.
The rooms are smaller and the light is different.
The cat has gone, maybe forever, and the neighbour's dead.

And every piece of furniture hates us
for being left alone. The plants won't give us their generous
blossoms. Every machine is reluctant to work.

Neglected homes take revenge
when you want to make a picture album
of your holiday. They call you traitor in every corner of the
photo.

# Intensions

Carrying all that was left of yesterday's memory,
he participated in the silent morning procession.
Sun was shining on the serious faces
of those en route
to throw away the last empty bottles
into the big green bulb, the cathedral for sinners,
where all the drinkers take their turn
and he said goodbye to the beautiful castle on the label
where he would have loved to live a little longer,
he admired the nice purple coloured stain on the paper
before the sound of crashing glass
brought him back to the rain that started to fall
into another grey period of sobriety.
The walk back home was full of good intentions
but the shade of red wine will always be his favourite
and this was not the last of his processions.

# City

Black coats pass me,
people move in the opposite direction
as I am going upstream
through this river of indifference
that smells of dog and travel, nicotine.

My limbs are gone, now only my eyes find a path
under tall buildings that are falling over
in the puddles showing blue sky.
There is no sky. This city
has taken from me what I knew to be real.

An old man stands still in the middle of a sunbeam
and plays a violin, some coins are shining
on the red velvet of the violin case.
His music is eaten by police sirens.
His smile is fading into a skeleton's grin and I run.

My feet fly above the grey pavement,
all the faces the same zombie,
and noise increases. Then
a traffic light. Red. I feel the air
come from passing cars.

A child smiles at me from a backseat.
Inhaling fumes, I move again.
The city swallows me but will spit me out
as soon as I can find
my way back to the station.

# The Secret

Has she ever left this house
where no matter what season
no flowers seem to grow
and thoughts don't show in laughter, not ever?
Did she once leave this place,
this street? This room?
If so, not in this century.
She has been there for always.

Framed behind her window glass
the widow's face is showing. She stares,
portrayed in stillness she is watching
how slowly the snow is covering the street
in glistening smiles all over her buried memories,
and she smiles too, or so it seems,
overlooking other winters with piles
of corpses that she can't forget.

Her image stays untouched, is centred
in the red bricks of the house
that her father built
over a hundred years ago
and where her mother died
after her seventh child was born
and where she herself cried, mourned
silently over losing both her husbands.

The street is white now
and her hair is grey now.
She's always there. Maybe she died
and told no one that she had done so
and there was no one else to tell about it,
so no one knows.
She could always keep
a secret very well.

# Wisdom

wise old men know this
going for a pee at nights
sleep is much better

# Time

He tells me the names of the flowers
growing on our meandering road,
their petals too pleasant for picking,
and he shows me the flight of the geese
above us, in silvery sunlight.

He does this so gentle and trusting.
What is love or not? All that matters,
he's patient while I keep on asking.
The more as he teaches of living
there are more questions coming to me.

We walk hand in hand on our journey,
the lines in his face are deep rivers,
all his tears are ships sailing to sea,
his eyes reflecting past and future.
My companion in life he is: time.

# Winter Idyll

a winter flower
life emerging through the snow
no sunbeam shows up

winter proceeding
hoarse crows find food under snow
all in blue darkness

a lonely cyclist
air running through his hair
no finish to reach

layers of snow conceal
wounds of the bicycle tracks
a broken flower

a dead crow in snow
run over by ignorance
tears of the black birds

satisfied cyclist
proud to have challenged winter
no respect for life

nature revenging
ten black birds come to his house
beaks puncturing tyres

# Bloody Christmas

I could stay where we are
hiding from snow and be fine,
no need to get up, if I didn't feel
how the tiny, thin glass splints
of the broken Christmas tree ornament
that was over fifty years old
enter the skin of my hand.

We could have that happy feel
as if all is well for a moment
because of candles
spreading their yellow light
and outside it would snow,
if you were here too.
It is warm here and all would be magic.

We could see smiling faces
in each little fragment
of the broken tree-ornament.
But for now I am content
with just the thought of you thinking of me
while outside winter is making things worse
and blood drops are falling on Josef.

# The Moment

This frosted moment in the afternoon,
you watching the grey sky,
the Russian poetry book in one hand.
Snow stopped falling,
a cat standing still in the street,
the low hanging sun behind the clouds.

No curtain is moving but eyes are fixed.
You don't blink. We hear no traffic,
no wind, an all over silence
is awaiting the inevitable:
the encounter of the new postman
and the neighbour's German Shepherd.

# Heathen in Church

On heathen days we might be blessed,
as we have no religion, you and I.
We dwell in churches
to seek shelter from the rain
but find tears in our eyes
as we are not alone here.

The people who once prayed
under this roof, between these walls,
linger in a crowded way, unseen.
We feel the cold damp sadness,
not from the rain that falls outside
nor from the mould. They are the prayers.

In desperation, voices whisper, beg, and stay,
a prayer for afterlife to give them hope,
and then they suffer till their death
but they are heard beyond their graves,
beyond their time. Beyond belief.

We seldom leave an ancient church in joy.
We seldom cope with such abundant misery.

# The Pretender

There is a comet coming
and if we rise really early
in the dark, cold night,
we might have a chance
to get a glance,
to see this ball on fire,
a coming piece of hot ice from afar
pretending to be some kind of a star.

I doubt I want to leave my bed
as from description
I think that we already met
in a bar some years ago
and his name was Harry.

# A Caring Woman in Winter

There is no telling how long days will be dark,
depending on weather, calendar, and mood;
she is knitting a sweater, the sort that he wears
on days when the Pole air enters the house,
the arms by now three times the arms of a man.
This makes her feel good. Though he tried,
there is no stopping a woman in winter who cares.

# Writer

He says he is working on a book
and cannot be disturbed. For weeks
he has been lonely in his attic room
and every now and then a curse
is heard, a sigh escapes,
but the rest is silence.

Sometimes the window opens
as he throws out his thoughts
on paper sheets that flutter in the autumn air
away to some far destiny unknown,
and weeks go by
and years move on
and he's still there. The writer.

# Sunday Surprise in the Seventies

Your mother smiled with charming hate each time she let me in.
She said that writing stories was lying and a sin,
this after I had told her
I wrote fiction.

At the end of every meal,
she would pick someone from her clan
to read the bible. I'm glad to say
that it was never me.

After the meal, during prayers,
I wondered where I would begin to peel
the paper layers off the wall
that stood between us.

I should commence above the dark brown clock
that hammered headaches every quarter of the hour,
night and day.

I tried to understand
the after-dinner conversation
but there wasn't any.

We had to sleep apart, me in your room, you in the attic,
but you came back at nights, our breathing kept on hold
while we could hear the others
freely breathe.

On Sundays we would wait until they went to church
so we could make belated love.
One day the minister was ill. Your family surprised us
returning home too early.

But then they were surprised as well
to find us naked in the kitchen, erected
in the early morning light.
You spilled the salt and I looked back and laughed.

And every Monday crows would tell me
that I did not belong and should go home
and every Monday they were right.

# Garden Tea Party

They sat with innocent carelessness
on the thin designer chairs
that in their elegant invisibility
made the chatting ladies seem
two floating female Buddhas but with hats,
who by some religious miracle
were above the rules of gravity,
until the weight of one of them
caused a break in their almighty faith,
hence showing the designers mean depravity.

# Waiting in the Hospital

They keep pushing beds with people
into rooms they never come out of again
and a baby is crying.
This is the house where life meets death,
and where bright Disney balloons
fill the sadness in the Central Hall.
To die and the last thing you see
is a waving Mickey Mouse. Hallo Saint Peter.

# I Met Rumi on the Ferry

I met Rumi on the ferry,
he was seasick all the time.
We hadn't left Harlingen Harbour
when he started to look pale
and he asked me—
I mean: he, Rumi, asked me!—
for some wisdom.
I told him to get a bit of fresh air on the deck.
"Fresh air is the miracle of transparency," he mumbled.
He looked outside, it was raining.
"Then again, perhaps not."
He wasn't quite himself, maybe.

# Deep Thought on the Ferry

all our ancestors
no matter what profession
once they were seamen

# Rather Knackered

I rather heard nothing than beat,
rather the sea than a band,
rather the day crack in silence
than with rather loud noise from the street.

Knackered and rather at ends,
I rather saw bed as in sleep,
rather a rest than to dream an illusion
rather be sure than to seem in confusion.

But all this has changed, rather by you,
that I rather listen to music at times,
rather hear people about than hear none,
that I rather feel life coming through.

I rather dream on while I can,
I rather live fantasized lives,
I'm rather in doubt what to do,
rather leaving decisions to you.

# Inspection Day

We were sitting in the classroom,
the most horrible boys in front,
the most silent girls in the back,
and the nervous teacher told us
it was now Inspection Day.

After some delay
he, the man from the mainland,
entered and we were numb with fear
as he was to decide
if all was well in here.

The school could well be closed
if we did not behave; hurrah for that,
of course. We were not worried
that the school would close.
The sooner would be better.

But she, our teacher, was another matter,
the nervous little spinster,
in her twenties but already an old maid,
we did it all for her, now didn't we?
She needed us. We knew.

We crossed our arms becoming one and true:
the perfect image of a nice primary school
with bright children, silent and God-fearing.
Then the most obnoxious boy
threw up his midday meal—oh jeez,

he had been eating macaroni ham and cheese,
his mother's fault, she was a lazy cook
so the other mothers said, well mine did anyway—
all over the important school inspector's
expensive black bright, shining shoes.

Teacher fell out of her role. She went all loose
and gave the boy a smack around the ear.
This made the silent girls go cry.
Their sobbing was all we could hear until we got some hope:
"Is school going to close now, miss? Oh please say yes!"

"By all means no!" Inspector said.
He was so rude we thought as
he did speak before his time, now didn't he?
"To know you lot would be outside
is more than I could bear!"
We sang the hymn of the good shepherd
in the way we'd been instructed
and he left. His shoes were sticking every step.
He firmly slammed the door.

We watched the mess that was still lying on the floor,
now flattened by inspecting feet. It smelled of sour illness.
"He couldn't help it, miss," a high voice said all in the back.
"It was that fucking macaroni!"
And Teacher starting crying; she now looked really small.

We were not bad. We were not bad. We were not bad at all.

# The Old Chair

The wood is infested by worms that
ate themselves perfect round holes.
Imagine living therein, your brothers
and sisters as neighbours, tunneling
to meet each other on rare occasions,

eating some more wood thus creating
more space. But to die in flames, what
cruel fate, why not leave that old chair rot
until the worms move out. Until the wood
is gone and they don't live there anymore.

# Going Vertigo

Between me and my early death was just the colour grey,
showing through the glass on every high-tech level
in the hotel building as the elevator rose.

Then gravity tried hard to nail me down on the
transparent floor.
My stomach turned, I knew for sure I would be dead
really soon,
the earth so far away from me, this was not natural at all.

Was this a one-way trip? Already I saw birds that flew
looking like angels.
Was it the prelude to a nasty, fatal fall?
I closed my eyes and waited for the bang.

"Here we are," I heard a voice.
I had not seen this man before,
when had he come to join me on this certain voyage to
our death?

"Madam, wake up, we've reached the ground floor now,"
he said.
I had been up and down this tower in ten minutes,
they seemed much longer than my life had ever been.

I stuttered something, and ran out the door.
I won't go up again, that is for bloody sure!

# Confession of a Would Be Sinner

My last confession shall be that
of a would be Catholic,
making the priest blush a little, I hope.
I certainly would want it to be
a sultry kind of whisper,
inappropriate, X-rated, and unsuitable.

His ears should be red,
and even the wallpaper of the room I die in
should shiver, but whatever I did wrong,
it would be forgiven
with a magic spell and ointment,
that is the best part of it all.

Now I need to live up to it,
if I have time, for to have this last giggle,
become a good God-fearing Catholic
in order to get that priest.
I need to prepare for my death-bed in appropriate style,
and contemplate sin for absolution.

# The Last Assembling

Once we are dead,
the information that has entered our brains
during the years we lived,
all the whispers, flickerings
and music tunes, the quarrels,
some colliding trains we saw on the TV,
and bickerings, the mathematics,
critics, manuals, the poems we absorbed,
every shopping list we read,

the Coca-Cola logo, the first-time sex, all other times
except those we forgot, and each commercial that was on,
think Spic and Span, Spacelab leaving Earth,
the daily dairyman, newspaper adds,

rude conversations that we had
and labels that we read, our fear of spiders,
war and hunger,
the memory of wallpaper in mauve,
a puppy's waggling tail,
the views we saw starting at birth,
the horrid pains that we had to endure, and joy

assemble

on a windy quay of a deserted harbour
where grass grows in the fading stones,
and go on board a ship no one can see,
to take them to a continent
the size of Africa
but somewhat more up North.

Or after death our minds get lost.
Who can be sure.

# Nightingales

The new day stutters as you rise, light flickers.
An old movie, life is showing off itself outside your window.
In the shape of some old woman memories go through
your head.
Trees are swaying as in trance, their trembling branches
worshipping tangerine sunlight. The larks, your friends,
are gone, you miss their song.

The street is shining emptiness while rain falls hard,
the branches lost their leaves already,
their dance becomes macabre.
After a coffee all seems peaceful for a bit,
and new is good, you say;
the sun rose as a flower.

You could be fooled so easily, go back to bed
and lured into some other dreams
postponing what must come. Procrastinating it.
But then in unison some crows
hack down the morning silence fast.
Why stay, you cannot do this anymore.

Where is it that nightingales go,
when they are old, to die?
This hurts your ears, this brings you down.
And worse: you've seen it long before.
You know this day.
It is your last.

# The Thought Collector

She secretly collected thoughts
like they were priceless post stamps in an album
or rarest animals in an exotic zoo.

From the moment of their birth
she kept them in a cage
and called them her sweet babies.
They never met anyone else, she would not have it.

She always feared the window draught
might make them fly away
if they should come of age.

No air, no light could enter
through the hatches of this house,
and pot plants perished in the dark.
She started having coughs herself
and died an early age.

When she was carried to her grave,
out of a cellar room a thought emerged,
the only one that had survived her mind
as all the others suffocated long before.

It trembled as it went outside.
This was the best thought she'd ever had,
a strong one about honesty, original and bold,
but it could not survive in light.

Before it was about to speak
and tell the mourners of their cold hypocrisy,
it fell down on the earth,
it moved no more, got trampled,
and what remained of it
was blown into oblivion.

# My Life Compares Itself to a Hangover

In the early hours after a blacked out night,
my life opens the curtains and asks me how I am feeling.
I don't remember having invited the skinny weasel into my bedroom
so I ask what it is doing here,
where I am all private part before I put on something decent.
"I have seen you worse," my life replies.
"As your life, I need to make sure you are not too happy about your actions of yesterday evening,
from about eleven till three a.m."
"As if I want to know," I moan. "Get lost for a while."
"I am like a hangover. I shall give you a splitting headache
and you shall regret every breath you ever took
between eleven and three."
"I take you up on that challenge and ignore you," I suggest.
"Like I do with hangovers."
"You had no alcohol last night," my life nags on. "Why is that?"
"I am living sober these days. You should try it sometimes."
"I can't be sober, I am your life, I need booze to give you inspiration."
"I don't hear you. And now you mention it,
you haven't given me much that I need lately."
"I shall make it up," my life promises.
It slips into bed. It puts an arm around my shoulder.
"Let's be pals again. I shall give you entertainment.

Come on, I have been with you all along,
even if you were not happy with me. I am your buddy."
"You smell of sewer."
"You compare your life to a sewer now? That is rich."
I close my eyes. My life won't leave me.
It whispers sweet nothings in my ear.
"Okay. Tell me then. What did I do
between eleven yesterday fucking evening and three a.m.?"
"You had es ee ex."
"Pardon?"
"You and that fellow. The one sleeping next to you now."
"My husband and I had a romantic encounter. So?"
"I am your life. I do not like you to be happy. Not like that."
"I know," I say. And now I see a tear there.
"Come on, old fool," I say. "I know I am often angry at you.
But look how you have treated me in the past."
"Hey, there are other lives a lot worse than I am."
"I know. And I wouldn't trade you for the world. Feeling better?"
"I want kissies."
Sometimes your life drives too hard a bargain.
I give it kissies and it falls asleep.

# Darkness

More or less completed dressing
after a nice encounter on the sofa
we watch each other
looking for the thing
that used to make us smile.
I can't see the love no more.
More or less the same
as we were before but in another mood
we take each other's hands,
walking on slowly.
We move on until we stand
where we so often stood yet we don't see,
we must keep looking
and find a replacement
for the freaking blown fuse
in the meter cupboard.

# Her Husband Is in Hospital

"I gave you seven sons,
every birth a fucking nightmare,
you always too drunk to call the midwife
or help me into bed.
I got them all on the freaking sofa,
and the stains never went out of the fabric.
All sons have your features,
all of them drink with your speed
except for Ronny who joined the ballet
and who gives me roses on my birthday
which was a hell of a day for my mother
who loved dancing,
but after her eleventh child
she could hardly walk anymore
let alone cross her legs.
She would have liked Ronny
as he can do a split
so don't be too hard on him
for hitting you with that spade
after you called him a flipping faggot.
He didn't mean it in a bad way
and the doctor said
you might still get some feeling in your spine.
Imagine that."

# Miracle

It was a phenomena when his wife stopped talking altogether
and instead of making him her black burned meatballs
she just stared as if she had seen enlightenment or a ghost
down the road.
People were surprised and called her holy, they only
whispered in her presence.

When after a month she still sat there in silence
without touching her tea nor her Weetabix, her stout, her
gin and tonic, her muffins, her diuretics,
they worshipped her for this miracle of complete abstraction
as she was holy no doubt and people claimed they were
healed by her stare.

Then this snotty boy from across the street noticed
how she was falling apart, smelled like a dead rat
and was it not a bit odd
that she had not taken a breath for thirty days?

Thank God the priest who came by every day
took the little pest home
where the sinner got a good spanking
for his disruptive behaviour.
Are flies not creatures of God as well?

# Observation

The immortal politician lives in this house where I live too,
we share rooms and bed and food
but the books he reads are thicker, his words on an average
are a syllable longer, and he is the owner of a dark blue suit.

I once put on that suit and it looked differently on me.
So he must be made of another material than us mortal souls.
I watch him. I make notes. I see that he is not the only
one of his kind.
Sometimes there are more of this sort in the house.

Thus I have studied the species of immortal politicians.
They are almost like us, but when it comes to discussions,
they like to win as if their lives depend on it
where we just like to talk. They make the nicest stews and
love.

# Clean

Someone told me my soul needed to be rinsed
so I took it to the dry cleaner's
who put on his glasses and examined the fabric.
He could not guarantee
that my soul would not shrink in the process.
I then took it back home with me, stains and all,
and put a vase on them so they won't show.

# Listening

Piano tunes fluttered out of the window
and we children stopped playing to listen.
Who lived there? We never saw anyone
but soon we were told not to enter that space.
We walked on in the brightness of summer.

One day a black car stood in front of the place,
few people were gathering dressed in black.
A funeral shuffled, the house had died too.
The quisling was gone, the unseen traitor.
We grew up surrounded by different music.

I walk near that house many years later.
Though much has happened to windows and walls,
his name is still of whom we don't speak.
The rain cries over lost shame and fear
as echoes remain of piano tunes flutter.

# P

Now I am talking to a coffee mug at five a.m.,
thinking of the night before.
Nights have ways to make things worse.
But reality came just in time
for some overdue adjustments. An early rise.

Often good ideas join the dark of night.
These days I tell them to get lost, I need my sleep.
They take their attaché-cases and turn their backs at me,
I hope to memorize some of their truth
but can't be bothered now to lift a pen.

Today I shall not try to be
a better soul, only a coffee drinker
who worries about rain and disappearing socks
and why it is that all you do when I am dozing off
is going for a P and waking me up to say so.

# Aftertaste

If your mind falls apart again
in shattered figments of a wine drenched eve,
keep your head up well.
Do not drown in the toilet bowl. Not yet.
This too will pass like kidney stones.
Bereave your hangover of untrue memories
by drinking water from the tap. Get sober.

We have been there my friend,
we all have met each other
in the gap where you have been,
between the party-flavoured fantasy
and the taste of moulded paper in the morning.
It's where the truth lies buried.

# Nights with Minds of Their Own

We tell most nights that we can do it:
close our eyes and start to sleep.
Some nights have minds of their own though.
They linger in corners, hide behind curtains,
or already have one foot out of the door
but hesitate to leave. A sense of duty.
Aware of our faults, they observe reluctantly.
They know all about our sad misbehaving.
They decide to keep us company
till dawn opens the window,
and grin at us because they know we can see them
but not keep.

One night had an understanding with me.
He would come back every evening
and watch over my dreams, keep them in control.
In return, I would not whine about lost sleep.
Some months ago however he told me
he needed a new challenge in life
so he went out of my bedroom
long before it was dawn.
Left between darkness and light,
I was back in the womb of pre-existence.
I was without night. Midsummer.

About to close my eyes this morning,
I noticed that the night returned.
He had missed me, he said, so we made up.
Now I sleep in his arms
and he whispers old poems in rhythms of rain.
Like most nights he tells me
that I can well sleep.
He makes sure my nightmares stay out of the bedroom.
He still has a mind of his own though.
Will he stay, I'm not sure.
I try not to whine.

# For

For those who went
with no return,
let's burn a candle,
share a memory,
a thought.

For those who went
will always stay,
let's think this way
as every candle
loves them.

Forever thoughts
return to us
in candle light,
in memories
relived.
The best of life.

# Passion Fever

After the wooing, the wining and dining,
he decided it was about time to get laid.
After all, he had bought her flowers and bonbons
and he got nightmares of all he had paid.

He knocked on her door wearing nothing but passion
while neighbours were watching in shock and delight,
she looked at him asking if this was now fashion
and then threw the door in his face for the night.

There he stood, very naked, with four blushing cheeks,
he was desperate now for a cover
as he all of a sudden felt like one of those freaks
who get too carried away pleasing a lover.

So he took down an American flag from a pole
and wrapped in that fabric he walked.
But he didn't get far, the poor passionate soul;
being sad, he had no idea he was stalked.

"What are you doing with our native flag?"
angry American tourists were screaming at him.
"Give back our pride, you ugly old fag!"
He escaped by means of a jump and a swim.

Wet and all naked he came home during dawn,
expecting nothing of life anymore,
but there she stood, all nude on his lawn,
more pretty than he ever saw her before.

"I have been thinking," she said, "and agreed:
I can see what you mean by being all naked.
It is not the clothes so much that we need,
so here I am. Leave it or take it."

"I take, I take!" our hero said gladly.
"Lie down and let me just show you my love!"
By then however the dream ended sadly.
He woke up with a cold, and a nasty dry cough.

# On Hot Days

On mornings when husbands sleep with their wives
while the hard rains are gusting the windows,
who has a new thing to say of such lives:
old beds that squeak of soon to be widows.

On afternoons when the children stay home,
no mom sees more than they're willing to show.
Kids would much rather leave town and just roam
on such days; they can't leave and they can't go.

On evenings when wives put food on the table,
the family sits in silence to eat,
and no one can move, as no one is able.
Days will go on so, disgusted in heat.

On nights when all wait for sleep before death
they feel the air of the devil's own breath.

# Ha!

Get rid of imperative poems,
those that tell you what to expect of life,
burn them with passion and watch
the flames stamp on them,
let no one tell you what to think
nor what you should feel,
and never listen to voices not yours.

# Word to Ponder

If possibilities are such
that they can keep me busy for some days,
the angles and the different ways,
the pros and contras;
live this or live another life,
all captured in this little word,
then thank you much
person who created it
to open new eternities:
I mean the miracle inside this word
called *if.*

# Create!

Choose new words every day, lift
thoughts out of their tight crisp packings,
hold them to the light
and watch them lose their weight;
so much to view from other angles,
seen in different mirrors now
the cobwebs are removed.
Open the box. Receive the gift.
Create!

# Losing It

I sit near a crow and think what it must be like
to have wings, to leave gravity for what it is,
to fly over sea and land and sea again:
it would mean excitement to me, a dream,
but for the bird it seems not out of the ordinary.

We look at each other, creature to creature,
depending both on food and water,
mortal, fragile, and a lot of what we have in pairs:
two eyes, two legs, so much alike we are
in most important matters.

The crow may read my human mind,
and wonders why I don't use my arms to fly.
I show him how I try, I flutter,
moving arms quickly up and down
with no result.

The crow beside me laughs and flies away,
only to return with two companions.
"Watch that human," I can hear him say.
"She has wings like dead tree branches."
Inadequate I stand corrected by some birds.

The noise of a helicopter right above us
suddenly scares them away into the woods
making me feel triumphant
though I know I have lost it today
in more ways than one.

*Ina Schroders-Zeeders*

# Extraction

They can replace all your body parts
with artificial, improved copies,
or you never needed them anyway.

Gone are your teeth, appendix,
a hip, a knee, a heart,
gallbladder, what have you,
and you live on, you are the same
but better. More prepared for eternity
as all the plastic and metal
will last longer than the organic stuff
that is originally you.

One day they shall invent
the immortal soul and then
you will be happy with science.

# Harbour Men

Eyes that look dried up,
leathered skin faces
that are salted barriers,
hardened and silent:

Men near a harbour seem to look the same
wherever you are. Surrounded by seagulls.
Blue anchors on their arms,
and they smoke. Or they chew tobacco.

Sometimes they laugh about something
that happened a long time ago
that they tell each other every day
adding a bit to the story each time. To make it better.

One by one they don't return in misty mornings,
one by one they are forgotten, but the story gets
better by the day, until they are whispered myths
themselves
and the last harbour man walks away into damp.

# Sunny Day

When clothe lines fill, a tiny tit
lands on some jeans that seem to fit
his ego as he sings for me.
Too bad he doesn't care a bit
of what I did, as he does shit
and makes my work a mockery.

# The Cycle of Life

I watch the Tour de France for the landscape.
The hills, the mountains, the castles go by.
After a while I wonder about why
saddle soreness doesn't seem to exist
for those skinny little fellows in bright
coloured Lycra. I watch them race in spite
of distance and heat, they move like robots.
Outside, the old man's cycling up the dune,
same speed as he's always done, the tune
he whistles says he is not tired yet.
He needs no yellow sweater to feel good,
he only cycles to get where he should,
and when he's home, the reward kiss he'll get
is always from his wife. I wonder who
is better off: the runners like they do
or him, the old man on his daily round?

# The Taste of Fruit

You eat strawberries
that grow in my garden
there
in that corner
near the Christmas tree
where we buried two cats.
You say they taste sweet.
I shall not mention the cats.

# When We Were Three and Four

We tried to see where our fathers were,
as we were standing in the mud of the beach,
and I would have taken your hand
but that seemed too intimate.
Your father and his ship at that time
was somewhere at the Mediterranean,
mine at the Baltic, but we were convinced
we could see them there, over the dark blue
of the North Sea, as some ships were passing by.

We waved, you and me. You called for your father.
He shall bring me a doll, so you said.
I could not say I was looking forward
to seeing him again, he was not even a memory.
Like all things in nature, the fathers came and went
and there was no telling when.
Our feet had sunk in the mud so we freed them
and we ran back to the towels and arms of our mothers,
their red bathing suits as reliable beacons.

# Summer Heat

If we put the heater on
warm, our feet against each other,
we could pretend that it is summer,
well it is, but it's a bummer.
Let's just put the heater on.

Look, the neighbour's wearing mittens
and the scarf he got for Christmas.
I shall make some nice hot soup,
let us hug and then regroup.
Let's just put the heater on.

Took my winter coat downstairs,
oh how nice that knitted sweater.
I heard someone saw the sun,
they say summer has begun;
let's just put the heater on!

# To Be Two Cats

This day won't need much to improve,
there's already light at four in the morning,
I've got coffee, a read.

Two cats, with eyes closed and probably purring,
are rolling over the pavement outside,
catching the warmth of some early sunbeams,
then falling asleep on top of each other.

They let the blackbird be ignored
so he can sing his morning song.
How much more can a day need.

Finished my coffee and my read,
I close my eyes and am just that:
a cat or two in the warmth of sunlight.

# Doing Dishes

Her worry moment is doing dishes
when her children pass her mind one by one,
every dirty plate another problem
she rinses quickly. The crockery floats,
tea cups seem boats on a foamy ocean
but she won't get distracted. She rinses.
The knives are the first to come out shining,
stains can go if the effort is thorough.

She sees possibilities. Another school?
Next the spoons and forks emerge brightly too.
But the plates need a soak. Her thoughts ponder.
Money is tight, she will be creative.
Ideas of how to make money come by.
The water spirals its way in the sewer,
she is done, she had a good think. Some new
dirty cups already pile up in the sink.

# Chaos

Eventually all you said will fade
into the orchestra's practice,
the cacophony of the universe,
every statement you made
torn apart by screaming fugues.

No one will ever remember too
that you said something at all,
but you will have said it. That
they can't take away from you.
It has been said. It has been done.

The sheet music is left behind.
Your words melt and all is blown away
but one sentence will remain
somewhere in someone's mind.
It was not in vain. She must have heard.

# Child's Play

We had planned a moment of silence
to underline the end of our relationship
when we were four years old.
It was the first break-up for both of us.

We wanted a ritual.
We sat in the sand, back to back.
"I shall not marry you," he said.
"I shall not marry you," I said.

Then we went on with our play,
making big deep holes
all the way through the black blue sand,
and emerging water sealed the deal.

# The First Mate's Daughter

I was child and played on the harbour quay
of a foreign town where people were poor.
A boy showed up, we had no words to say
but he signed that we should go for a tour.

Climbing a China clay road with this stranger
from the cliff I could see our ship in port,
above us sea birds that spoke of danger,
there were some ruins of an ancient ford.

We watched the water slowly serpentine,
beneath us all looked pleasant, greenish land
that we pretended was now his and mine.
I didn't know him, yet he took my hand.

We were a princess and an Ivanhoe
and now and then he was a cowboy too.
We played without much talk but with much show.
He took me back when he thought I was due.

I made a friend that day when I was five,
a boy named Sidney showed me where to play,
a memory I want to keep for life,
of when the world was safe. A golden day.

# The Landing

It feels as if the land is in my skin,
the sand has entered through my pores and eyes,
the people who have lived here, live my mind,
and clouds they saw, are now above my head.

The green of May, the brown of fall, the snow,
they saw it all and heard the sea rage on,
in the same way as I do now. The salt
that stays upon my skin, is what they tasted too.

Now underneath the sand the earth has moved,
as different times have overwhelmed the strand,
new dunes emerged, others are washed away.
Not everything remains, as life goes on.

Then as I walk the beach, a trembling breeze
comes rolling over waves into my ears,
the wind then goes and in the light of dawn
a ship with sails is floating above sea.

A stranger out of nowhere finds the shore.
His footsteps disappear as he walks on.
He is a father, he might be a son
who once was lost. The island shall be his.

# The Town with Many Statues

A young man on his first trip as a mate
left his ship to see the famous town.
The streets were simmering, the sun went down
and gardens smelled of home. He met his fate.

She was most beautiful, her hair was red,
she only charged him what he could afford.
He forgot that he was needed back on board,
and in her room they made love on the bed.

Then when the morning came and light was hard,
he woke up knowing that his ship had sailed
but to his heart this love he felt, prevailed
as it was love and had been from the start.

He turned to her and shivered, she had changed
into ugly, soars and lumps, all skin and bone.
She looked at him and turned him into stone,
another statue in the town arranged.

# Yet

Worn out lies the street before me,
the empty eyes of the houses
stare sadly over my head.
This is the town where the future has ended,
now trees are too dry to have leaves.

A piece of bright coloured plastic
is flowering one of the dead branches.
The wind won't even howl here,
shadows won't stick,
there is only the silence of crows.

Yet
I see a butterfly dance
as if nothing happened.

# Almost Forgot

In this, the season for nightmares
and spiders, various shapes of horror show,
strong blown up ghosts that haunt in wee hours
and long moulded memories growing new fungi.

But the nights are short now, so
I rise early to beat them to it.

Eagerly I go downstairs to see
the sun rise if I am lucky, and forget
what I just saw in the figments
that linger in darkness.
Over coffee I am almost back
to the real world where all is well,
opened are the curtains. I am set.

One spider that escaped the dream,
came with me from the bedroom floor
to keep my feet some company,
it looks as if in need of shelter, or
still shocked from its own nightmare
that might have been about the likes of me.

Daylight creeps over the floorboards.
We wait and there she is, the sun.
The spider and me both enjoy, *aha!*,
the warmth, the light. We bond a bit,
we nearly hug, but then I shriek it far away.
Almost forgot: I am afraid of spiders! Duh!

# Village

The village is asleep when I sneak out
to see the silence lean on houses,
some chimneys smoke, but people are still in their beds,
a quiet damp of warmth hangs over all those rooftops
and under every rooftop a different dream is dreamt, a
secret kept.
Somewhere a child is being born. And someone dies.

And then the first dog barks. Another follows soon.
A car is starting engine. A ship blows its low whistle
and the church bells ring. The new-born cries.
Seagulls are screaming loud above this all, the noise is now
a steady.
This is my home, where clotted silence overrules the
whispered voices of the night
until it's dawn
and children start their lives whenever they are ready.

# March of Horror

When words can't say the horror
that paintings cannot draw,
and music has no notes for it,
what use of rotten memories
that come to pester us in dreams?
Just when you think you have forgotten,
come marching skeletons of long ago.

Some memories are not our own,
but haunt us as they need to be remembered.
When words are gone, and tears dried up,
where silence screams of what was done
to others. They come to tell you what you know.
They should stay in the memory of all.
Cold wind is blowing over Bergen Belsen.

# Secret Lives on Bus Rides

There's wastefulness in all time lost
of moments where the mind seems blank.
You can't remember every second of the bus ride
home through traffic lights and cars and frost.

Yet in flashes, chained sharp fragments,
wherein we live our secret lives,
when genius meets our make-belief,
is beauty of a hidden love in figments.

Those thoughts that are forbidden thrive
on what we sense or what we should let go.
Still everything is soon forgotten, gone
as we step out the bus at half past five.

# Poems About Love

I read poems about love and it was not so for me,
stuff about the moon and the smell of roses
didn't ring a bell.

A poem about love for me describes the waiting
for the moment to pass the butter from his hand
or light that is singing when he opens his eyes.
How a stone dies of loneliness
before the day decides to end life in silence.

Maybe I should not read a poem to the letter.
I must try to smell the sweetness of the moon
and be blue in the light of roses.

# Birds of a Feather 1

I don't see
that they are different:
doves and pigeons;
in the light of dawn
they are all
heaven-sent to me.

My guess is pigeons
are on their way
home to sleep-in late,
after painting the town red
the night before,
while doves need to
take their white feathers
to the cleaners
early in the morning.

# Crisis Conference

I watch her hands as she talks;
she gives every word she speaks
about the crisis a gesture.
Her hands are birds in a ballet,
thoughts on wings in dusty sunlight.
When they have taken a bow,
the stage is a worn out table again,
and the sun is gone.

# Foreign Esses

They're whispering
in foreign esses
so sharp they kill a fly
above their heads.
They must be Germans
or from another country
which such sharp esses
in their speech. English maybe?
I try to sleep.

I don't want to know
what they are saying.
They hiss some more,
they never stop,
they have so much to talk about.
Before the train has reached its destiny
I dream of steam engines
and snakes and esses
that are sharp enough to kill a fly.

They're whispering in foreign esses
so sharp they kill
a fly above their heads.
They must be Germans
or from another country
which such sharp esses
in their speech. English maybe?
I try to sleep.

I don't want to know
what they are saying.
They hiss some more,
they never stop,
they have so much
to talk about.
Before the train has reached its destiny
I dream of steam engines
and snakes and esses
that are sharp enough to kill a fly.

# As the Moon Does

Few items mean so much to me as the moon does, or
a sunrise, a pet's photo, smiles with crackling lines,
the smell of tea, contours of old castles. Cathedrals,
relief after a storm, surviving all.
Clean sheets. Our family. Standing by the sea.

A hand on a shoulder. Our sons. Your letters.
The silver and green shamrock hanger I got in Dublin.
A Christmas tree. That happy feeling on a ship.
To be alone. Write. Read, or days in May. Violins.
New notebooks. Your body, and the verb *to be*.

Chocolate and train trips, walking, old cities, Norway.
Perfume, days after giving birth, getting published.
That I can see. A good bed after a long day. Fresh morning air.
Daisy chains, sweet white wine, an April shower.
The blue of the sky. Snow maybe. Sense of being free.

# Souvenirs de Gravelines

One voyage we came
in a French harbour town
named Gravelines
where no one lived
who had not been
affected by war
two decades earlier.

Street dogs sadly walked,
tails between their legs,
brown grass was growing
on doorposts with no paint.
There were no children
in this town.

A man cursed me in Flemish
for not giving him money
when he asked for it.
I had none to give.
He said our ship was doomed.
I was a child and I believed him.
Why were the children gone?

The cheerful cook went into town
to get himself some souvenirs.
He showed them later,
as we were already at full sea,
they were hanging
on the wall of his cabin
next to the pics
of his brother's children,
he himself had none.

He had bad dreams there in his room.
He changed. He never smiled again.

The souvenirs of Gravelines
that he put on his wall,
they were old scars,
the memories of battle
and screams of those in doom.

# Not with the Program

Howling ours between midnight and dawn,
a storm is raging outside; we snug up together
and I try to remember making love,
but whilst doing so, I dream I'm squeezing
a kiwi in the bloody blender. It is not a kiwi.

Trying to make healthy breakfast at six,
the storm in its worst, still close together
we remember making love all right,
but whilst doing so, I think it is a
kiwi I squeeze in the blender. It is not a bloody kiwi.
But I did come close.

# White

the world is white now
it makes my mind
a sheet to begin
my morning with
a new write

white's promise
to give choices
of what is,
what to leave out
or whom

but nothing
decided yet,
all is still
white

# Horizon Birds

Always there is the horizon. And never it is making sense.
It is no line, but just an abrupt ending,
a fence between the world we know and all that lies
beyond.
Yet I see a line. My mind wants logic in this too grand
overkill of space.

I want boundaries for my world. I need a lined out place.
Some birds escape there, flying out of what can be
imagined
into another world. I envy them today. Forever gone
and out of sight, while I am standing, in reality, now lost
to them.

# Grave Stone

Of what it's made, I am not sure, some sort of stone,
the letters are all washed away by time, and moss
is growing where his shoulders would have been
if this was him, and he'd be standing, but it is not.

And he just lies here. Underneath, his bones.
They all took shape that we are not aware of.
But it's relevant no more, how bones and hairs
are lying and in what specific order. Now, who cares.

This is a grave. The moss has taken over death.
But if you're silent, you can hear the grass sigh
softly. Think of it: this sure must be his breath.

# Verbal

Pardon me for being verbal.
I've tried silence, animal and herbal,
but I always bounce back verbal
so forgive me that I speak and talk and say.
I could not do it any other way.

# Under Skies at Night

Under skies at night, all is different
for the mind: more alone we feel,
surrounded by cold shades, old scents
while unknown distances approach us wildly.

We seem smaller too, the sounds we hear
are stronger. Animals make noises of another kind.

Hours seem to last much longer in the dark.
Maybe differences occur because we should be dreaming.

Nights are made for thinking of the day.
Once we've done so, they just slip away.

# Yet to Read

They look at me with hard accusing eyes:
the unread books, the old ones leaning on each other's covers,
Stendhal's *Le Rouge et le Noir*, Simone de Beauvoir, and even Nabokov
are silent witnesses of my guilty laziness, my idleness
(and how they stare at me!).

Procrastinating I have built a wall of words
that never saw the light of day,
they are the fortress from within
I think I know enough. I know so little, though.
I only know De Beauvoir and Sartre once were lovers,
but on two different shelves, they cannot even touch.

They look at me, and sometimes I just turn them face to wall,
as I can't bear the look of so much right when I am wrong.
One day I'll make it up to Proust, to Marx, to Lewis Carroll even.
How can they know I have a life somewhere.
Anyway: they shouldn't stare, it's rude!

# Invited for Tea

I think I've said all that I am able,
after an hour of small talk, my jaw
wants to freeze in midst of conversation.

My hand goes for the cake on the table
but the family dog puts his paw
on my arm. Won't let go with persuasion.

The people say what a nice dog it is,
and it's starting to drool all over me.
while it's grinning at me with those dentals

I want it gone, but it's starting to kiss
my hands. Of how to behave well, I see
it surely does not know fundamentals.

And it's only half past four, so I see.
An hour to go to be civilized.
Not sure I can stretch my smile much longer.

I say thank you to one more cup of tea
before I shall get that dog brutalized
and I don't care that it's so much stronger.

I watch how the hound is eating all beef
and drinking from half full glasses of beer,
getting a maniacal look on its face.

At last it is time to gracefully leave
and to lie what a nice time I had here.
I think I'll never return to this place.

# Nights

Maybe I should not stay in winter nights
outside in silence, while everyone sleeps,
to linger long, watching the cobalt skies.
Maybe I should not try to understand.

Indoors is warmth and when the door is shut
I can pretend the world is just our house.
But here, in magic snow, I'm more at home,
in winter nights under the cobalt skies.

There are more questions in those winter nights
than stars, and many shine, but why they do
will always stay a mystery, unsolved.
I stand under the cobalt sky and wait.

# Moon

For the first time I watched a full moon then,
without thinking of love and romance much,
or other clutter of my human brain
that had nothing to do with moon or such.
I watched the moon and thought how nice a cup
of hot chocolate would be now. Right here and when.
My hands were ice. I looked above. Hot chocolate.

Maybe because this is the thousandth moon
or more, that I don't feel of moons the way I did before,
or maybe that you never felt the same.
Another moon with just another name
would not do. My hands were ice. Hot chocolate.
For the first time I could watch a moon so full
and only think of hot chocolate in a cup.

# To Love

To love is said to be a verb in grammar.
As soon as it gives trouble, it's not true,
'cause when it makes you blue rather than happy
it is not what you want in life, but through.

And giving it away, why don't we love for free?
Love, since it is a noun, is plural too.
How many times we love, why should we count them.
As long as love is honest, it will do.

# Home

This is my home, but home could also be
there, where I've sensed my true belonging.
For me, I am not sure I need this place
where I have always lived, where I know how
this longing for another place might be
all but too real. This is my home. For now.

# Cortege

Some moments linger in the after mind,
their impact can be so immense:
a funeral procession in the mist,
the kind where no one seems to be alive,
that's moving slowly to the graveyard's fence,
the eyes that stare away into the past,
the thin old man who's burying his wife,
the silence now, as she is no more here.
We think of our death, perhaps, or fear
the moment when it's time to go at last.

But in the cortege, see, there is a boy,
who looks at life without a single doubt.
He pinches roses from the coffin lid
and full of joy he waves one in his hand.
His smile is making all the fog clouds go,
before the sad procession comes to end.
We find the burial went well and calm.
Some moments linger in the after mind,
their impact can be so immense:
a funeral procession in the mist.

# His Brother Wore Lederhosen

The sand was not good enough for building castles,
so they said.
Something to do with the roughness of the grains.
Every time we built one, it collapsed, driving us mad.
And then he came. A silent boy, just carrying his spade.
He was from Germany, and blond.
He had a very German name.
Each time a grown-up spoke to him, he bowed, he often
shook one's hand.
His brother wore some Lederhosen that would shine.

He didn't speak with us, but started digging early in the day,
and by the time 'twas noon, revealed what he had made.
It was a castle like we never saw before.
It was so fine! We were amazed. We lost our speech.
His glory didn't last for long;
the tide came and his castle washed away.
But from that day, he was the master of the beach.
Unlike the brother in his Lederhosen that would shine.

# Welcome to the Island

Another ferry is bringing in strangers
and we shall await them while we stand on the quay
not looking at them directly, but from a corner.
They are new here, what do they know to expect,
the Germans, the campers, the schoolchildren.

One by one disembarking now,
look how they fear us,
and with good reason
as we are the locals,
we know where the shops are,
but we won't tell them.
We shall point them into wrong directions
and we shall make it rain all their holiday long.

# So Tired Is This World

So tired is this world already, tired
of the steady waves and breezes;
they cuss this Earth, that is so
tired of indifferent abuse.
Of always giving birth.

Above the monotone repeat
of day and night, which is
the beat of battered hearts
that have no love to give,
we live, we die. No fuss. We lose.

So tired is this world already,
even rain has stopped.
The sky forgets to cry
for the loss of our planet.
It forgets to cry for us.

# Christmas Stable

The live Christmas stable got a cold,
so Christmas is postponed
till the codeine kicks in,
although it is believed by then
the shepherds will be stoned.

# Christmas Spirit

We listen all evening to carols that rhyme;
just a reminder that this is the time
to sit all dressed up for a large dying tree
with candles burning too dangerously,
and outside we can see some ugly cold snow
so we have no place to escape to or go,
we must sit it out together my friend
let's be glad that it all will soon be at end.
Pass me the calories, pass me the wine,
if we keep up the spirit, we might be just fine!

# Time 1

Time, we so need time, to be in, to live in, to heal in,
we see it on the graveyards, as there lives time,
we do need time desperately, we also hate it.
We find it in mirrors and in condolences.
Time grows on us, and makes us older,
as time is impatient, never waiting,
never showing any mercy at all.
Time is not gentle and soft,
never it is generous,
not to us.
Time brings pain,
sadness that lingers on.
It leads us to an early death,
or finds us looking back in tears
at sunny days when we're being happy
playing with a toy horse or a bright red ball.
Death meets us at the end of the darkest alley,
that's where we are when there is no time for us left.
Lost we shall be then. Gone. It always has the last word:
time.

# The Ferry Fly

The ferry has a fly on board,
that's trying to adjust
whilst flying on from port to port,
it can't escape, but must
stay in this space, detached from ground,
eternally, till death will make it dust,
and always homeward bound,
forever being cussed.

# Hibernatory Mood

I am in hibernatory mood today,
don't try to persuade me to go out.
I watch the street and how the stray dogs have their fun
while rain is falling, someone's gone to run
and I am put to stay. I put the kettle on,
no way we're going anywhere,
me and my hibernatory mood.

# Scent of a Wanted Space

I would have liked to keep this empty room
just for some thoughts, for drawing faces,
or to watch the view of goats
grazing on the dune, an empty room of possibilities,
with a table and a chair and nothing more.

But practically, the room is used for laundry and to store
(books and boxes), to give our guests a bed.
Only in my mind I have this room,
and in reality I hang the wet clothes there to dry.
I've grown to love the scent of fabric softener though.

# Heirs to the Bone

After her death, but only just, we relatives assemble
in what her house has been, her presence lingering
in furniture and cups, food stocks for just in case
a war breaks out quite near. "Who knows! Life can be such
a gamble!"

We touch her old bone china plates,
the ones with pinkish flowers,
we listen, we expect her voice still echoing
in all that has to be divided, how can we not feel shame
to go through what was on her name and now has to be
ours?

# Old Woman

She lived alone
in something of a house
with sand as floor,
a table and one chair,
no light, and she was old.

They called her witch,
she never left the door.
The others dared me to go in.
I entered, and she was surprised
to get some company,
as I was glad she didn't eat me all alive.

Once she had been somebody's wife,
now all she had
was looking forward to her death.
But how she smiled!
As if she knew a secret that
I had to earn to know as well as she had done.
No teeth involved, no there were none,
my fear had been in vain.

I went away for just a month;
when I returned,
her house was gone
and so was she,
so was her smile,
and no one told me what or how,
but every now and then,
for just a little while,
I see her face again.
Her secret not unfold.

# From the Land of Cuthim

Your arms stretched out,
the world that hurts
has been embraced once more by you
and once more all the planet's pain
was crushed against your breast,
and all the tears were kissed away,
but you can't carry
all the burden on your own,
you need to rest and let it go, shrug
your shoulders, leave, as pins and knives
are penetrating through your back.
Now it is time for you.

# Poultry

You look at poultry and don't think:
These were birds once,
wings and feathers,
they had distances to fly,
and eggs to lay in self built nests.

You see a chicken's carcass, legs, the breasts,
and think of food and gravy to go with it,
what wine goes best with duck or dove,
should we have two each, or is one enough,
but they were birds once that you plan to eat.

Maybe if hunters missed their goal,
by now this bird would fly over your head
and shit on you in every colour green.

# Standing by the Stone

The grave is waiting there but doesn't care as such.
I now and then wipe nature droppings from the stone.
The grave would be okay to be there left alone,
as graves don't mind about who's grieving all that much.

I come here for the blackbird's song each time I go.
He sings his graveyard tune that vibrates through the air
with thoughts and memories emerging everywhere.
It is a simple tune that all the mourners know.

In what he sings, I hear my father's laugh, his scorn,
and in the melody my mother's unsaid words
now spoken clearly in the language of the birds
and sounds I heard from times I wasn't born.

# Space

Sometimes when sea and air are almost one
it's possible to slip into the space between,
a moment lost in time, to be all gone
from earth and sand, and go to what cannot be seen.

# Timing

I serve eggs burned,
or not boiled long enough.
If timing is a virtue
then I am a sinner,
always too early
or hopelessly late.

The nice people already
have found all their friends
before we finally meet
and I am already gone
when you arrive at the party.
Timing is the worst part of my life.

# Poems Among Poems

There is a place where all the poems gather
for their annual meeting, their social affair.
They have a beer, a hug, and rub a shoulder,
another year older, some typos are showing,
now who found a partner, and who is still single?

With pain do they watch the old villanelle,
that no one understands these days as she mumbles,
getting more and more tipsy, till she almost tumbles,
then someone takes the old girl to the home,
while here in the café the others mingle.

The haiku, always the first to be silent,
as he is short in words, buys all a new drink.
They talk about rhyme, and how to omit it,
there's almost a fight, but just in time
a nice Shakespearean sonnet makes them shake hands.

They dance rather rusty, two free verses go crazy
and a tanka throws up, but nobody cares.
After hours, when the others have left,
two disputing sestinas still linger
and won't go home till it's already day.

So much to say in so many words.
Till next year, my friends,
and take care of yourselves now!
May the spirit be with you
and the sentences flow.

# The Moment We Made Gods

Outside is now a sky with many stars
that make me shiver in my almost sleep.
There's so much space that it's called time instead
and deep down underneath this, only us.

I wonder when it was that men looked up
above their heads to notice all those lights
which didn't fall down on the earth, but stayed
at nights, only to disappear in day.

It may have been when men just realized
there must be more that we don't know about,
as thunder made them sleep together close,
the loud and angry howling of a wolf.

I see the stars and feel I could make gods
from angry wolves and thunder in the air
and my respect would be towards the stars
as there they live now, looking down at us.

# This Borrowed Life

We live on buried dead bodies,
our houses built on those long gone.
On and on we reinvent life
till the crust of the Earth
cannot grow much further
into the sky.

We lie on top of each other,
smothering our reason with force,
sourced out remorse, giving birth.
While our children await,
they become us in turn
to do their part.

We shall be in their memories
till they too become soil and clay,
what will stay be our fate.
We shall be dead before
we're buried beneath them
like all who went.

# Not Yet

A day further away from birth,
I stare at graves I haven't seen in years.
Halfway here and neither there,
I feel the pulling of the Earth,
she wants my body to endow
what she claims is rightfully hers.
There's death around me in the autumn air.
How glad am I to leave this place. For now.

For now I'm safe as I can go,
aware of how, in some, uncounted, years,
one might stare here at my grave,
where weeds and flowers wildly grow.
Earth takes me back where I belong
as this is where we all end up.
It doesn't matter what they will engrave;
long gone am I by then. Let them be wrong.

# The Café Lieman

At night the fishermen from Urk would
drink themselves to happiness next door
in the café where they would sing and dance.

A bright and cheerful murmur reached my room
and in a storm, the men would drink till four,
to over voice the hauling wind outside.

Accordion and singing filled the night,
a woman laughed, some breaking glass, a roar
all covered by the turning lighthouse beams.

In such a cheer no fear of mine it seems
would last to keep me from my sleep; therefore
I slept, till all went back on board.

I heard their wooden shoes above the storm
then only hauling wind, the squeaking floor,
a hungry screaming cat, a woman's cry.

I've wondered much of how 'twould be
to be in such a night once more
and smell the chimney smoke and beer.

# Walking to the End in Rain and Hail

Some greyish funeral attendees
passing by my house,
while rain is hitting them and hail,
walk silently behind the hearse;
only the last one says a curse
but no one minds. This was his friend.
Old mates they are, and will be to the end.

# Frame Rate 25

The truth lies,
I suppose, in what there can be seen.

I know the world, as shown on my TV,
truth, in between the frame rate intervals,
finds ways into my cervix, where it stays.

A tortured Syrian child, the name Omar,
whose nails were torn out, lingers on my mind
then falls apart when a commercial starts.
Not waiting for the rest, I zap away.

From forecast on to football
to pruning of a rose, a cooking contest show.
A Ronny always makes me laugh.
By every second twenty-five
new images invade me more.

But when I go to bed,
accompanied by thoughts of life,
I close my eyes to find some peace
in dreams and fantasy.
The sleep won't come.

How can I sleep,
as in a corner of my room
Omar is watching me
with frame rate twenty-five.

# Rain on Graveyards

No graves can comfort us,
their stones remind us not of whom we loved
but only show that everything is fading:
their names, our memories now running thin
while everywhere the rain is falling on the graveyard
no graves can comfort us within.

# The Sake of Art

There is a poet living in my head.
It must be by mistake,
he may not have found the attic room
next door that is for rent.

He drinks a lot at nights,
keeping me from my sleep,
singing sobbing Russian songs
and playing Armenian music
on an instrument I don't know.

I am glad he leaves me alone by seven
so the stuff I need to do can be done.
But by the time I have my coffee break
he starts mumbling.

I can't do anything about it but write,
bring what he says into lines
and he doesn't pay rent
so I suffer tremendously,
all for the sake of art.

# Nature Wise

What is made by nature,
is never one straight line.
What tree grows like a human made pillar?
All whirls,
meanders,
grows in bends.

So my back is not straight.
I am made by nature.
Don't cure me.

# Rape Seed

The gods have lived here,
kings and knights at war,
but has this field
a name to remember
who owned this land,
this soil, where, so far
just yellow flowers
and a lonely tree
under the grey skies
silently wait
and nothing changes
when the wind is moving east?

The waiting land
has seen the secret sins
and bastard kin
working on these fields.

The seeds of rape
became strong sons,
lived farmers' lives,
died with no names,
and all remaining
as proof
of their existence
are these flowers.

Listen well: a whisper tells
the tale of this waiting land
when the wind is moving east
and nothing changes much.
But who planted these flowers
with this telling name?

# In Thoughts We Live

The web is a net,
a spider a fisherman
I said and you laughed.
Can you see in my mind
in my thinking what matters,
can I feel what you feel
through layers of technique
that I want to be
with you, nothing else.
Can you be with me
and tell me who was first,
the fisherman or the spider?

# Bone China

His horse and car came twice a week,
he would empty buckets of shit and pee
and smile without teeth
when I gave bread to the horse.

He would sing without words,
humming it was called,
but he was not allowed in the house
because of things he had done.

We watched him from behind the window
and one day I got him a cup of milk
because it was hot
and he was humming.

He killed a fly on his arm
and put it in his mouth.
I never drank milk
from that cup again.

# Meeting Again

I saw him when he was already dead awhile
so he apologized for being smelly
and he didn't take a seat, nor coffee
for apparent reasons, I didn't need to ask.

We talked a bit about what went on in life
and then he left, walked out the door.
So stupid that I forgot to ask his address
and where about he does hang out these days.

# Early Morning Thought

To wake up without
a hangover
dry mouth
memory gaps
and him
was the best way
to start
life

# Basic Weather Poem

Rise and look
rainy day
put on coat
find warm socks
look for shoes
go outside

rain has stopped
oh how nice
it is hot
go inside

take off coat
take off socks
summer shoes!
go outside

it pours now
go inside
just give up

go to bed.

# Flummoxed

I can take words for granted,
put them on my shelf
for dusty years to come
and forget they ever popped up.

Some words however
linger on the table,
I find them under the sofa
and in the fridge
next to the orange juice.

I need to do something
with words like that
or get flummoxed.
So there.

# Bloody Mess

Bloody mess every month
for years,
three weeks on end, forty days even,
cramps, thick blood lumps
of what looked like grapes
came out of me
and pink sausages
that didn't give me appetite,
lots of fatigue and dizzy spells,
pools of blood where ever I sat
and pain
so the doc gave me the birth control pill
and it worked.
But now I cut my finger.
Bloody mess.

Is there a pill for stupid?

# Why 1

I shall die before
I have seen most flowers
known to mankind
but all I need to have seen
are the daisies
in the chain you put in my hair.
They should be enough to
last me a lifetime.

Yet I bought a vase today.

# The Sound

From far away somewhere that day came sound
across the water of a quiet sea,
there was no breeze, no people were around,
there only seemed to be this sound and me.

What kind of sound it was, I cannot say,
the voice it used I never heard before,
it stayed awhile, then slowly went away
and never it came back to our shore.

But now and then, when I walk through a storm
and watch the waves that come and go in pace,
I wonder what it was, what kind, what form?
Was it a creature from a distant place?

As time goes by, the more it's out of reach,
that sound I heard, while standing on the beach.

# Be Like a Butterfly

The moment we are born, we start to die.
As butterflies should we be in our place,
they give to flowers when they know to fly
and make it art to do it with such grace.

From when we feel the earth under our feet
we know that there is more for exploration
enjoying every new day that we meet
and growing up we feed our expectation.

But for the butterflies we meet on our way
there's soon an end to everything they know
when pretty flowers fade in their decay,
reminders of the day they too will go.

Between the moment they are born and death
they cherish each and every taken breath.

# Goodbye (for N)

You were a part of me, my dearest friend,
I often shared your bad times as a child,
you were a tiger, just as brave and wild
and now I heard that your life had to end.

I'd been about these streets in other days
away from all that makes a mind a mess,
a holiday from feelings more or less,
of wandering inside this complex maze.

Though while I wandered, you were on my mind,
I heard your voice as if you stood right here.
It was your presence that, so real and near,
was surely of a different, stranger kind.

The mist came up, along a breeze from sea,
a salty smell reminding me of you,
the way the mist in May will always do
like when we both were children, you and me.

The foghorn sounded as a sad salute.
A gull was crying in a raucous prayer,
and all was gone, the mist was everywhere
as well as in my eyes. My thoughts went mute.

A moment there you were, a child again,
a silhouette against the hazy sky.
You lifted your right arm to wave goodbye
and disappeared before the mist turned rain.

# Night in the Attic

The attic where we children played our games
was where so many must have died before
forgotten people with forgotten names.

In summer I felt heat from ancient flames
in darkened days of winter there was more
of what the mind can't grasp, in shades and sound.

A hauling wind could speak of pain and fear
the boards would squeak when no one was around
while things got lost and never they were found.

The attic of my youth, now I am here,
what has it lost or gained in all those years?
I am no guest here, this is home to me.

I hear the dripping of the smothered tears,
a moving shade of someone's face appears
but who it is, I dare or cannot see.

I close my eyes and cover both my ears
yet hear the shuffling feet of those long gone,
a laughter and a cry then all is still.

I hear a car outside, the night is done,
there is no reason why I can't go on,
no harm returns and evil never will.

I leave the attic of my youth in morn.
The sun is warming up the earth and me
I feel triumphant for the new life born.

A last time I think of the souls forlorn,
for ever in the attic they may be.

# Logic

Most quests may start without a clue,
still the quests as such matter most.

Most raindrops fall into oceans,
some, though, might fall on thirsty land.

Most love is given for granted.
Thus love is the quest of raindrops.

# Landscape After War

The flowers seemed all gone, left the landscape bare,
meadows, ploughed by tanks, becoming muddy pools.

The swollen bodies, hastily buried into earth,
waited patiently where they were left to rot.

When guns knew they were done, silenced, rusting there,
birds returned to sing and also nests appeared.

The poppies all have grown, flowers from strong seeds
marking now the place of the nameless graves.

A brighter springtime came, sheep were giving birth,
all was moving on, the landscape soon forgot.

But silent blue are nights, with, out of shady weeds,
whispers from some souls are going through the fields.

This was before we lived, but through the fields we walk,
events that were erased, they happened on this ground.

What right have we to live not thinking once of them,
dead now because they fought where lovely flowers grow?

# Survival of the Fittest Heart

What you can survive, of what you die,
how come there is no line between them?
Some die insane of a broken heart
and others live on, through all of it.

Always a story has to be told
and the story belt grows on but still,
never we know how some can survive
and others die of a broken heart.

# What is Time

What is time,
it has passed where our footsteps ended,
and moved on to beyond what we can see.
Like in the red of the setting sun, we are never there.

We cannot grasp the mere beginning of it all,
we are somewhere in the middle of never and ever,
and we are falling deeper and deeper in the pit
that is time.

# To Being Fly

The first of flies has come inside today
and hits his head against the window glass
which doesn't slow him down, the silly ass,
who doesn't understand what's in his way.

The first of flies is in our room this spring.
We open doors to get him on the move
as his departure is what we behoove
but it won't go at all, the stupid thing.

The first of flies has come and can't get out.
We watch him loop, hear how his engine purrs,
but nothing useful to our mind occurs
to help him see of what it is about.

The first of flies has come, maybe for good
or for as long a fly can live his life,
it is his goal, his job, from nine to five
of wasted want, of never understood.

# Tree

By the time you're halfway in the street
your feet decide it's time for a revolt.
They just refuse to walk, to do their daily round
and so you stand there grounded and become a tree.

In all your arms the birds will make their nests
and leaves will grow and cover up your face,
in autumn storms will bend your branches deep.
You will not walk another inch. You are a tree.

# The Origin of Mermaids

Every month we women watch
our blood flush down the toilet
into the sewer on its way to the sea,
carrying the unused egg,
and we hope it will find a mate,
a sperm that escaped the laundry.
We give them our blessing,
we send them our strength.
Making mermaids is done like that.

# Where Warmth Now Lies

How grim are times at times
when all is black and white
and greyish, so much grey.
In time, after some time,
a less cold sepia will grow
inside the memory,
where warmth
now lies.

# Waiting for the Right Time We Die

Waiting for the right time we die.
Bridges are not built, hands not reached,
the moment doesn't come,
procrastinated in eternity
we die and all is too late.

# Droste Tin

I watch the lighthouse watch me watch
and think of Droste cacao tins
on which a woman stands, a nurse,
she has a tray in both her hands
on which the same tin can be seen.

The nurse who's carrying the tin
returns infinitely it seems.
She's disappearing in what can't
be seen by eye but is still there,
for ever doomed in her repeat.

I watch the lighthouse watch me watch
and think of Droste cacao tins
on which a woman stands, a nurse.

# Heroes

We sat and did nothing
and governments fell
and trains collided
and everywhere was war
but we sat it through.

# Comfort in Times of Grief

If it's draughty in the coffin
and your body feels a chill:
just remember, what a fun time
you would have now, as the will
at this moment has been read
and you left the family nil!

# Forget Me, Nut

Don't think of black holes now
but you do now, don't you,
just because I mention black holes.

Maybe you should close your eyes
and not think of me anymore.
Does this work for you?

Don't think of me when you eat
your horrid oatmeal
or comb what is left of your hair.

And never think of me in the bathroom.
I shall try not to think of you not thinking
of me in the bathroom too.

# Ghost

I feel cold breaths that pass my bones
as flesh and blood are there no more.
Now storm and hail batter the shore
my ribs are shattered, falling stones.

As flesh and bones are there no more
a skeleton I am to be.
So hard the truth has come to me
that nothing will be like before.

Now storm and hail batter the shore
I am no more, my ghost is not
the whom I was and you forgot.
I'll stay unseen for ever more.

My ribs are shattered, falling stones
that drift away over the sea
and no one will remember me,
my flesh, my blood, my shiv'ring bones.

# Night Delivery

I heard the doctor say: "If you jump a bit up and down,
the baby might come quicker that way,"
so that's what I did between contractions,
but not indoors, as then the floors would shake.
A house is not built for such drastic actions.

It must have been a strange sight, for those still awake:
a big-bellied woman, jumping in the early hours of night.
When I did so, I noticed my neighbour,
a man in his fifties, was doing the same kind of jumps
at the back of his home.

"To have my kidney stone pass!" he panted, "and you?"
I could only nod, out of breath, out of speech.
He talked about health while he started to foam.
"The best remedy!" was his final submission.
Well, we happened to have the same crazy physician.

# Nomads in Pain

It hasn't been an easy way
out of the deep. We came from far.
Bewildered we are till this day.
It hasn't been an easy way
and maybe we're not here to stay;
somehow we made it, where we are.
It hasn't been an easy way.
Out of the deep, we came from far.

# Islanders

When late in the evening
the tired ferry slowly enters the harbour,
rocking strongly there for the last time today,
after a rough sea journey,
all on board look weary and grey.
Silent people, nothing to do with glamour.

Been to hospital and back, been to family.
Been to funeral, nothing to mention,
so much to think and to worry about.
Hollow eyes that see no prospect.
Eyes in faces that have known each other for life.
A kind nod is all, telling the stories not needed.

Then the moment comes, where all are waiting for,
as the lighthouse shines a beam over them in redemption.
To be near home, to have made it again,
in spite of diagnosis, expectations, like so often before.
As a mother the light has been waiting for her children,
and gives a calming sign to guide them in port.

Some hidden smiles, this is the one
victorious moment in the day to enjoy,
now, late in the evening.
They all manage a hoarse "see you later"
when they step out on the cold quay once more.
Home. Now they are fine.

# Dream House

There is a house, there are houses,
in my dreams, in my nights I return to quite often,
where more rooms than needed
can be reached by brown stairs.
They are all full of bookcases, books,
and emptiness too, but have voids that excite.

Dusty sunlight does soften the years of grey silence
and comes in from milky glass windows.
To my surprise, always another room,
another door, another room shows up
every time when I dream, always another dream,
another house, but still the same feel of home.

A room for a child be, the possibility,
with old carpets and furniture, familiar but why?
Rooms for a thought, to escape, to explore.
There always is one more room available,
never that posh, and the ceiling all rotten,
but! To be there, whenever, to have that space!

In the abandoned cellar, lie, eaten by spiders,
remains of Buddha and other interesting thoughts,
resting in shadows, so useless in real life, but nice for a
while in case boredom might strike,
they are dead, among the vintage year bottles of wine
that nobody likes, but everyone treasures.

Oh this house. The friendly house, the secret home.
When needed, there is one more room to find,
that I love, that I know somewhere is,
but had almost forgotten, or so it seems.
My place to feel me, to expand, and feel comfort
is the house where I come in my dreams. In my nights.

# Meaning?

There is no reason in this quietness
when we eat,
it is not a quarrel prolonged
but interrupted for a meal, no
it is not, this silence has no sinister meaning
nor cause, no consequence, it just means, if you like,
that we eat.

# Today

Today you felt the sun as it was new.
It touched your face, it made you think
of womb related pre-birth warmth
and pleasures soon to come
as it is spring.

But see, the sun has set
in shivers of the sea
and soon this feeling
will be darkened by the night.
Not much on Earth is meant forever.

# Our Story

There is more to the story of us
than we have told each other,
than we have found back
in old family photos,
in our genes, in rituals
and sounds.

Hidden in dark caves and old riverbeds
some creatures live that we don't know
and where they started their journey,
or if they fit in that of our own,
remains to be seen.
Still we think of them and call them dragons.

Nothing we know of this
is true or false, as we can't judge,
there is no beginning nor end
and still it's a story.
We live in it, slowly turning the pages,
making poems about it.

# It

Nobody found it so far and many of us gave up looking
but it is there. Maybe the mothers will know it before
anyone else,
but it is there. Ask for it, hope for it, go for it.
Perhaps the scientist will discover it, and die with a smile
on his face,
but it is there. Be in it, feel in it, stay in it.
Find it. You are the only one who knows where to look.
And I don't know what it is either.

# The Deal

The eyes saw all, but look surprised
to see the reaper in this early hour.
The sunset not quite ready for the day
is mean enough to hold back on the dusty beams
that always were his reason to arise.

The reaper hesitates to make the crucial gesture.
There is still time for some negotiations,
so it seems. What is discussed, nobody knows,
but in the end, the curtains close.

"He looks surprised," his feeble grandson says
the next day when the mourners come
to shed some tears.
The reaper, standing in the corner, smiles.

The deal is done.
He will not come to get this child, not
for a hundred years.

# The Arriving of the Omen

I should have known the reason that trees died
in streets this man passed by, their leaves just fell
and clouds went darker, wherever he would dwell
while thunderstorms would put him in white light.

I should have known this season was all right
for him to spread on earth his sulphur smell.
While black crows flew across the old dry well,
a sudden silence came into the night.

The man had gone, now what was it he took
from our small village? No one dared to look.
I should have known: from then on, we knew freight.

# This Change

Every day the earth changes a little,
mountains move down or up, onwards,
rivers bend slowly in new directions.
Oceans take over land while deserts
expand their territories.

The noise of the seasons,
new life replacing the old,
squeakily this planet turns,
spinning faster than ever.

And all of this is happening
while you and I stand here
watching the sun set,
knowing it is not the sun that sets,
but the Earth changing
little by little. Into what?

# Ninety Something

Getting out in the sunlight
after a season in the old people's home
there she is, pushed by an angry-looking woman
who wears sunglasses and an expensive coat.

Her wheelchair is brightly decorated with balloons
and she is smiling. She made it through another winter.
"Let's go to the harbour!" she says with her birdly voice.
"I want to be close to the water!"

I am not sure this is a good idea,
as the expression of her daughter's face is changing.
"Yes mother, what a lovely thought!" she says
before giving the chair a big push in the right direction.

# Evening Shades

Now evening shades are entering the room,
a little later than the day before
(although that is not noticed much by who
lives here, and who just came in by front door).

They slowly move, take over the white wall,
the portraits, fading in oblivion,
see no longer what is here at all
(as if they'd care of what is going on).

And just when darkness conquers light,
when dusk gives in—the magic's gone
and all is night. The TV now shines bright.
The lamp switched on, the mystery is done.

Although the shades are leaving grounds once more,
tomorrow evening they'll be back I know,
to get the right that they've been fighting for:
their place under the roof, that they want so.

# It Is the Way It Is

It is.
The chosen road,
it is the way it is.

Is it the only way,
dividing destiny
and designation
each in its own
secluded section?

A road is just a way
to go or not.

Should one obey the tarmac
as laid out
or be a bird
and fly
regardless of direction?

It is the way it is,
and every road
leads to reflection.

# Images

I saw words
like little portraits
of noble people,
or they were
ballerinas dancing
and on their shoulders
always a good head
to go with it.

Some were arms
reaching out
for lines of perfection,

hands, pointing fingers, angry fists,

but only on good days
they became legs to stand on
for more than a sentence
in an overcrowded white sheet of paper.

# Words

Words are the keys to many a thought,
opening doors of the mind with their force.

They bring us to places we never sought,
entering spaces of night and remorse.

Words can be shared, stolen, borrowed, and bought,
so that we find the way to our source.

# Marrakech

Away from the triangle square,
the fuming Djemaa el-Fnaa,
where colours blinded me
and sounds echoed centuries
of everyday traditions,
I saw these eyes across the narrow street,
and earth, warm sand, now felt under my feet,
was needed badly as a token of reality.

I saw you stare again,
you were the begging child,
whose legs were broken to gain sympathy.

Your life seemed hell to me
but in your eyes reflected Africa, was life.
The smile you gave, showed me no desperation.
Your spirit had not gone, like mine would have.

And never I would go back home
as whole, as all of me.
A part of me stayed there, with you
a part of my own sanity.

# Children in a Graveyard

We looked for names in the graveyard that day
and found some, distant related be.
We dwelled for a while amidst the old stones,
nothing sad in our hearts and we giggled.

Then there she was, an old black, green-eyed cat
just staring at us, demanding respect.
The cat was so right that we silently left.
Behind stayed our laughter, in the graveyard.

# The Crow 1

A funeral was passing by my window.
In the tree across the silent street,
a crow was watching with content.
Then, for a moment, his eyes met mine. Asking.
I felt it was suspecting my near end.
I shook my head. "It is not time," I said. "Not yet."
Screaming sadly, the bird flew up and went.

# What Lies Beneath

What lies beneath, hidden by time,
captured in a forgotten thought
is ours to find, the reason we sought.

When our journey is uncertain,
sand is blowing over our track,
we must move on, there is no way back.

# Nehalennia

Was I the only one who thought of you,
Nehalennia, on this stormy day
when not only ships were sailing, passing through,
but also thoughts drifted, floating away?

Did someone else think about you, and who
you were, guiding ships from our island bay
going across those tempest waters to
shores unknown, uncertain in a way?

I saw you, watching the ships sailing too
from a cloud, on that cold stormy day.

# Grave Days

With every year that she draws to its grave
she dies more than she lived days on this earth.
The force of life, at times a tidal wave,
that threw her further away from her birth,
now pulls her back, giving her a new start.

She digs a hole to burry this year
in letters she couldn't send, and a card
to her lover. He will never be near
more than he was alive, in her heart.
The year is done and the grave is covered.

# Leningrad

Somewhere hidden
in the wooden salt container
that you bought for me that winter,
a smell of some sweet fungus
mixed with a cheap perfume
is waiting for shared memories,
the kind I hope you
will find somewhere too.

Keep looking for them
in the lines of old women's faces,
like those that folded
when she sold us
a newspaper in the Newski Prospekt,
"Pravda," which means "the truth,"
but we couldn't read Russian that well
so the truth never hit us.

Do you remember the taste
of my father's burning vodka
when everything was frozen?
We had chosen not to judge the world
covered with black spotted snow.
A cold war ended in the mean while
as we grew up, but where,
my friend, did you go?

Somewhere hidden
in the wooden salt container
is the winter when I first saw
life as lovers know it.

# The Poem

The words kept circling,
butterflies of your mind,
lines and stanzas sent to me.
I tried to touch them,
out of reach they fell down
in front of my feet
in an order I had never
expected truth to be
and for one moment
I understood, I understood!
Before the draft
took everything away.

# Pin Up

You look smart, dark grey trousers
that you insist are black
and a new light-blue shirt,
the kind that is pinned up in the package,
under your blue jacket that you think is grey.

We manage to find a tie with a paisley design
somewhere in a box with other old stuff.

Minutes before you leave to catch the ferry
I discover a remaining pin on your shirt,
just above your fly.

While you are being politically important
I smile, feeling almost important too
as the woman that noticed the pin
before disaster.

# Why 2

There is no one else now,
and hollow are the lines remembered,
the funeral has left you standing in a vacuum of time.
Where the priest said words suggesting
a fine eternity for the beloved,
now is air and only air, yet you fail to breath.
This day has meaning that you cannot grasp.

No one should allow the traffic on the nearby road,
a dog is barking in the distance,
builders work at a construction site:
indifferent noises interfering grieve,
as if to make a point that life goes on
when it so clearly doesn't.

Some arm around your shoulders tells you
it is time to leave the graveyard now.
You want to tell the person not to bother,
as you don't know now how to walk,
let alone that you could leave,
but when you look, there is no other.

And rain is pouring, a sympathetic gesture
from the unseen sky.
Down in the earth, the bones are resting
in dead flesh that soon will rot away.
Should you not care then?
And, ask, for God's sake, why?

# To Choose a Dream

This heaven that she found
is the bush her father planted.
It carries fruit, raspberries
that will rot before they ripen.
She loves them even with the insects
living in there, as this is her childhood,
how it should be memorized.
She learns her history by heart,
in children's songs and kitten's play,
a swing and siblings running,
laughing through a summer garden,
of a big and friendly house,
and never there is rain,
and never darkness.
She picks the memories to guide her
further down the road back home.

# Lake View

There were no answers in the lake,
the water was too deep to take
a look of what is down there.

The silence though seemed well aware
of strings and grabbing bony hands;
all evil memories of you.

Under the surface then appeared
your cold and cruel eye to have
a stare of great contempt at me.

I took a branch to hit the eye,
it drowned, a wild and open scare,
in circles of the troubled water.

I turned away and said it all goodbye.

# Diving Up

Of other person's mornings I know nothing,
I cannot see what happens in their minds
when sunrise gives the best away of colours,
and people going to their work,
what do they think?

I see the blue, first sky in over three weeks' time
and white of cloudy floating stripes:
a lake that's upside down.
I cannot know of other people what they see or think.

They might be wondering why I am hanging upside down
out of my bedroom window
to see the lake the way it should be seen.

# Morning in April, 2014

The red morning has butterflies dancing
the tango. Looking east, all seems blood now.
You praise the day and I close the curtains.
One should never look east before coffee
nor worry of "maybe" long before lunch,
you say. What will happen next? I worry.

# Despair

"This used to be my brain, now is a graveyard
where memories rot in grey and brown shades.
Once I could remember what they were about.
I do not mind. My mind has done with me."

She stares over the street that she can't name.
Her room is on the top floor of the building
where windows never open. Black birds
smash themselves against the glass. Despair.

"I need a spade," she tells the nurse who frowns.
"I need to dig the graveyard up."
Her medication is adjusted. Another black bird
kills itself by wanting to get in. Some years go by.

One morning her bed is found empty. A window
is shattered, glass everywhere. But no sign of her,
she seems to have disappeared. A note says:
"Gone to do some digging." And a black bird screams.

# This is an Island

"But this is an island,
so there are limitations,"
I say. He just doesn't understand.
To him, an island, be it human,
be it sand, is a challenge.
He wants to see if waves
are really made of water
and people made of bones,
to shelter their cold hearts
when he tries to hug them.
He runs over the beach
with no other goal than running,
making friends.
Golden Retrievers are like that.

# Why Winter Weeps

There was a Winter once that mourned a love
and darkness came for months over the lands.
Her name was Summer, with the Sun above,
murdered by the evil Autumn's hands.

Now she was dead, sad Winter covered her
with snow, reminding him of Summer's light.
Home in cold and frost he buried her
where she should lie forever in his night.

Spring told him how to bring his love to life
so she could live forever more on Earth:
if he would kill himself, saved would be his wife.
Thus Winter went, and Summer got rebirth.

But Summer heard about his sacrifice
that took away the only love she'd known,
decided that she needed to be wise,
as sister Autumn wanted Winter's throne.

"If he could give his life for me in love,
why not do the same for him each year?
A few months living surely is enough
and through this deal he also can be here."

So every year after her light has shone,
she kneels for Autumn just to give her life
and darkness comes to tell her time is gone.
But Winter therefore always mourns his wife.

# Deceit

Days end as started.
Faded blood stains,
reminders of what went on
here during day,
under heaven's surface,
below the belt,
beyond humanity;
in luring shades of red,
just as cruel
in its lies and deception,
lovely to our hopeful eyes.

# Finding Truth

I hear a farmer talk of cattle
and his voice becomes
the heartbeat of life
once I forget to understand
what he says; the melody
is like a fisherman's orating about
the best places to find herring.

Somber, honest, and deep is the sound
of men in the midst of manure, or on ships
covered by the shit of seagulls;
that is where truth can be found.

# Be a Dreamer

There are dreamers at the seaside
who will never sail the ocean.
There are ships that sail forever
on a sea that has no coastline.
Some have lost their crew, abandoned
they keep searching for a harbour.

There are places where you salvage
what remains of thoughts, reminders
of ideas you had, ambitions,
long forgotten loves and wishes;
in those places you will find them.

Some birds fly with no directions,
some stay near the fishing vessels,
others know where they are going;
all will gather at the harbour.

Be a guest once more in harbours
where the fishermen are dreaming
over days when they were sailing.

There are places near the seaside
where you need not leave the harbour.

Be a dreamer coming home there.

# II
# The Road to England

# The Cliff

The cliff, where suddenly this country starts,
is home for herring gulls and weary ghosts;
all cruel reminders of mortality.

Who jumped from here to live no more? The shore
is about death, despair, and loss, but herring gulls
and weary ghosts, they understand each
other well.

Their cries are heard over the
beach, then followed by St Mary's bells.
Here England starts, where sea's at end. The cliff.

# Behind the Cliff

Don't go alone to what's behind the cliff;
take a path that leads you anywhere,
but don't walk on as you are unaware
that many drowned where thousand seagulls live.

Some ships have never made it to the shore;
don't go alone to what's behind the cliff,
as many drowned where thousand seagulls live
who didn't know the darkness of this shore.

# The Stone

There are no stones, no rocks in this landscape,
just sand and what grows on sand. Water. Mud.
Once abroad, I feel the power of rocks,
cliffs, ancient ground to belong. I take a stone.

I take it home with me. Questions arise.
Why take a stone to travel home with you.
How to call a stone, a pebble, a rock
that doesn't belong and is indifferent.

The sand is softer, bends more, shapes and blows
while the stone is constant in existence.
I took a stone away from foreign shore,
now it is resting on the windowsill.

The stone has moved into a landscape where
only sand rules. But it feels right at home.
There is a grey stone now in this flat land.
Forever the same. Never blown away.

I found a reason on a foreign beach.
Sometimes we need to go away to find
what's left behind, what matters in a shell,
in seaweed, a grey feather, in a stone.

# Fish

Why are they angling on the pier,
their gear well taken care of:
they know of fiberglass and throwing line,
of spods and rods, harpoons and hooks,
they only use real feathers,
and have the best of bait,
real flies, some worms, some dough,
and they wear fancy wellingtons
and mackintoshes in rain, in wind,
in autumn fog, for days, for nights, forever,
enduring cold and loneliness,
in misery and pain, in need,
their newspapers soon soaked,
beer running out, their cigarettes
all wet, and damp and swollen are their feet,
arthritis and bronchitis felt,
and fish won't bite, they get provoked,
and worms escape, and oh how horrible
it altogether smells,
when only twenty yards away
there is a cosy fish and chips?
With haddock on a sale and all!
Because they're men.
Why else?

# Whitby Museum Artefact

They have a hand here that is mummified,
it once was of a criminal, then chopped.
I watch the black thing and am horrified,
think how the cut went, how the hand was dropped.

The man explaining has a ponytail,
he spends his time in these museum rooms,
where all the facts of life are shown on scale,
a history of this old town resumes.

The fingers point to where the exit is.
We leave, the rain just pouring now,
and on our mind that man, the hand, once his,
what happened to the rest of him and how?

So nice the coastline lied before our feet.
We had no clue of what we were to meet.

# Downton Abbey

I could live in Downton Abbey
sometime before the Great War,
preferably not as servant, but even so,
I would love it there.
Carson and me we would be allies
from the day of my birth.
If I happened to be part of the upstairs clan,
I would give the maids a raise each year
and days off to go to the fair in Thirsk.

I would never think of money,
my father taking care of that.
Men would be interesting for conversation
but I would almost become a spinster.
Then fall in love with an artist
who painted my portrait
and was suspected of killing someone,
then have his child when I was in my forties,
causing a scandal but they all loved me anyway.

In the end, I would elope with Carson.
We would live in France
the rest of our rich lives.
And then of course all ends in 1914.

As a servant, I would fall in love with the son
and he with me, and we would see each other
secretly. In the end of course I would get his child
just before he dies of consumption
and it would cause a huge scandal.
I would elope with Carson,
who then married me
to make the child legit, the age difference
not bothering us at all.

I could live in Downton Abbey
but only before the Great War.

# The City

On a big screen
placed on the wall of the Carriage Works Theatre
the people of Leeds can see the Olympic torch
as it is carried and welcomed with cheers
throughout the region.

The square is empty though.
Just a Japanese man and me
have taken seat on a bench
and we watch the golden owls of the Civic Hall
watch the screen without a blink.

He knows a nice haiku about owls
if I am interested
but just when he starts, in Japanese,
rain is starting to fall.

I listen, get wet, more confused
when he wipes tears from his eyes,
I seek for shelter.
Golden owls, the screen
and the homesick tourist remain
on the Millennium Square,
belonging there.
The City.

# In Henrietta Street Now it is Noon

While colours seem a different shade
in Henrietta Street now it is noon,
as always you can hear the sea.
You're here and not a day too soon.

Here, buy a book in Grape Lane where
the shop is piled with old and new.
The colours seem a different shade.
The swing bridge gives a golden view.

In Henrietta Street now it is noon.
A ship is entering the port,
as always you can hear the sea.
You wave to those who are on board.

The Swing Bridge gives a golden view
and gulls are sitting on a car.
This is *away* for you although
you feel at home, and not that far.

Belonging is a word you find.
You're here and not a day too soon
to find that all is still in place
in Henrietta Street now it is noon.

Yes, coming back was needed much.
Belonging is a word you find,
but soon it will be time to go
and leave this mystic place behind.

# At Six P.M. Somewhere in March

To be in a place you don't know
at six p.m. somewhere in March
and smell unfamiliar food being cooked,
you suspect the sun to go down soon
but how soon—you don't know,

to find it is time for a drink
in a pub, then make a stroll
not too far out of town

where the shades make you think
you have been here before,
that you lived here, you must have,
but they have forgotten your name,

and yes the sun sets right on time
in the sea when you reach the shore,

to be there in March
watching that moment,
to be in that moment,
that is what you came for.

# These Men Have Been Here Forever

These men have been here forever in town,
they must be over a hundred or more
in number, and they know all of us well.
Slowly they walk through our streets in the night.

They must be over a hundred or more
as they were here when our grandfathers lived,
knowing them all and their parents as well.
They talk about wars no one remembers.

As they were here when our grandfathers lived,
how come they don't die like everyone else?
They were in wars no one remembers now.
In dark clothes they stride and peek through curtains.

How come they don't die like everyone else?
These men have been here forever in town!

# There Must Be Ways

where no one knows just where we are
there must be ways that end somewhere
no road would ever go this far
where no one knows just where we are
deserted tarmac with no car
as if no drivers ever dare
where no one knows just where we are
there must be ways that end somewhere

# Almost There

The moors have been quiet
but I expect eyes,
sighs and whispers,
movements swiftly in the heather;

I don't mind dwelling here at night
regardless of the weather,
I stay here sitting by the cliff
as I feel well at home in restless darkness.

# Yorkshire Wise

Here forgotten dreams
come back to live with me
and keep me company
in my last hour.

I hear the waves
roll on the beach
to bring pebbles
polished smoothly

for no reason.

Old grave stones rising in the mist
each with a faded name,
they tell me
I have been here
only to be forgotten soon,
like the bones once buried here,
the people no more missed and rotten
but loved by those who
carried them up the cliff to rest.

My mind has picked out scenes like this
that I love best to get me through the brightness
of this
my last morning
as light is much too reasonable,
unkind to wanderings or ease and never right.

I close my eyes now
dusty sunlight
is invading the old abbey,
I feel at home
and sleep forever
here in peace.

# Whitby

While they await a sudden luck in bait
the gulls are pondering at the Battery Parade.
They've got it made. They really have.

There is the admiral, the herring gull
with most authority,
watched by a keen and swift
female Kittiwake
that knows exactly where to lay her eggs
(somewhere in the cliffs over Jump Down Bight).

She smiles at him
and he examines both her legs.
"Nice bird, but not my sort," he reckons, and he's right.
As if she cares. She yells that he can go to hell.

Then something else comes up:
a little boy is dropping chips all over
and while he's crying 'bout this loss of tasty fries,
more gulls come in from beach and ships
and how they scream to have a feast
at his expense and eat his chips.

But then he smiles, forgetting he's the victim
of sheer robbery, as his mother gets him
an ice cream and a hug. Her sweet perfume is lingering
until the breeze takes it away to sea.

Lovers walk along the quay
and can't make up their minds as where to eat:
The Pie and Mash, the Magpie, or at Harry's?
Or maybe just a pint will do, or two, inside the Fleece,
outside the Dolphin, or another pub, or give it up and
settle for a view that is amazing.

The sun is changing sides,
from east to west
across the river Esk,
while a pinkish sky
is reflecting in the harbour.

Hence another day went by in Whitby.
Nothing much happened,
but everything mattered.
Night can come to close shop.

# Segedunum

We went to see the Roman fort
and found only the very ground
on where it once was built to last.

Our feet were shuffling through the earth
and industry was all around.
The River Tyne sent us grey damp.

And then, from nowhere did he come,
I saw this Roman soldier stand
amidst the non-existing stones.

I felt his homesick eyes that stared
across the river over land
where hostile tribes would live and wait.

The last he was, of all the men
who long ago here did exist.
He had kept watch, as he was told.

He raised his hand in a goodbye
before he faded in the mist.
The Tyne had taken him for good.

# Driftwood

The North Shield piers let go of me,
two arms, a hugging-like farewell,
as we sail on into the sea
and England once again
is over, soon to be a memory.

As in a last hasty embrace
the piers stretch out for me
while driftwood finds its way
from River Tyne to sea.
Maybe the wood will wash ashore
the island where I live.

A raindrop moves down over window glass,
the waves are all that we can see.
The ferry now is on its own, the sun appears
above a sudden deep-blue sky
and standing on the deck
I close my eyes after the last goodbye.

# III

The Road Through Nature

# Storm

Emanating havoc from the tempest waves
the storm makes landfall in the autumn night,
the loudest noises ruffle through the bending trees
amending thoughts and alternating purposes, creating fear:
a branch becomes a hanging tear, a rabbit tries to flee into the sea.
Then all is quiet in the woods, the storm is gone.
Under the rubble life emerges to go on.
The woods have changed their ranks
and storm laid down its anger.

# Abhorrence

There is abhorrence in the landscape
where no flowers grow to hide the truth.
Beside the graves your tired soul keeps post,
unseen to watch us move for hours
towards the new dug hole
as one we loved the most is gone
and we must bury and move on.

The tree trunks stare at us,
their rinds are tortured faces,
disapproving of our thoughtless tred
disturbing as we pass their resting places.
Nothing is said. The rain falls
on the leaves above us and in a million shots
all hope of resurrection is destroyed.

Appalled the grass knows
that it will be crushed under our weight.
This is the date that no one wants to have.
The grave we lay you in smells of decay
while all of us throw in a handful sand.
A scream comes from the earth;
she takes you back the way she gave you birth.

# Instinct by Nature

The morning sun shines hazy,
some swallows make a nest,
a cat wants to attack
and tries his very best
but falls asleep in spite,
before the crucial leap
then gives it all a rest;
the feline is too lazy.

# Trees and Old People

What trees have to endure in storm and hail!
The branches choose: to bend or get ripped off.
They are not weak though, finding strength this way.

Old people smile; they understand the trees.

"We are here just awhile. Let fate prevail."
What they had to endure, and do not speak
about: trees know, as they move with the wind.

I know so little, even less for sure.

# Swan

The thought came, a swan in my day,
landing on the surface of the lake
corrugating the water, shaping
endless flows of new thoughts
in the cool and green haze
of the silent morning.
Then she spread her wings
to fly away again, leaving
me calmer as the water forgot.

# The Tree That Said Farewell

The shivering roof tiles abhor and moan,
the storm-struck house is shaking to the bone,
while water from the sky falls down, and blown
away are well-loved trees, hardly full-grown.

Then suddenly the wind falls still and we,
not hiding anymore, come out to see
how bad it is, the damage and debris
and what became of our old apple tree.

Who would have guessed blossom met our eye,
such lovely white, and out of season, why
it started blooming now, in winter's high,
with branches full, why did this tree not die?

A miracle it seemed, that spring like tree,
but it was a farewell, too good to be.

# Geese Flight

Inhaling crisp air coming from the Pole,
I watch the geese move in their restless wiggle waggle
bound for the voyage and to fly away.
They feel the cold increasing, almost frost.

The sun shines low and blinds me,
with both eyes closed I listen to them call
as they start leaving for the South.
Sun cannot blind a bird, you say.

I don't want to believe you.
To me they close their eyes
the moment they leave ground. You
seem to know more about life than me, though.

Here all grows dead, the nights now cold,
we must have been forgotten,
I haven't heard from anyone. December grey
has slowly moved up in the woods.

I cannot blame the geese for leaving.
If I could fly, not blinded by the sun,
I'd follow them into adventure. If I could fly
and drift as free as feathers of a bird.

Today perhaps they'll go away
and no one knows their destiny,
what makes them go there anyway?
Above us hours of ruffling wings.

A feather zigzags slowly down, a promise
to return in spring, or maybe a goodbye forever.
You try to reach for it but it gets lost in mist.
You cannot catch a feather in freefall, I say.

# Autumn (In Three Languages)

Here in the Northern Hemisphere
the sadness of death
softly slides near the water,
where the church finds itself
lost in dense mist.

Autumn is the season of harvests,
of wine and potatoes, but also
of dark, dreary colours, yes, here
I only recall
the pain and the black.

# Automne

Ici dans l'hémisphère nord,
doucement la tristesse du mort
se glisse au bord de l'eau grise,
où l'église se trouve
perdue en plein brouillard.

L'automne est la saison des récoltes,
du vin et des pommes de terre, mais aussi
des couleurs foncées, sombres, oui, ici
je me souviens seulement
la douleur et le noir.

# Herfst

Hier op het noordelijk halfrond
sluipt de triestheid van de dood
zachtjes tot aan het water
waar de kerk zichzelf verliest
in dichte mist.

Herfst is het seizoen van oogsten,
van wijn en aardappels maar ook
van donkere, sombere tinten, ja, hier
herinner ik me enkel
de pijn en het zwart.

# The Alien

I walk in nature where I am an alien,
my clothes, my thoughts are fabricated
by chemicals and other people's smart ideas.
Nature never made the words such as I think.

Unisono the crow hacks in my spine.
I am the stranger in the forest, or the long-lost child.
And even treading her on careful, clean bare feet,
the earth resents my being here and sends me spiders.

We are not one with trees and birds,
only observers of how life would be
had we not dwelled from Adam's garden,
had we not found a way out of this murder scene in green.

# Autumn Gala

In October lace
as the occasion is gala
nature appears
trees wearing trains on their dresses
no movement yet
all wait for the dance to begin
the moment the intruder is gone

# Amazed

The latest of the mist that lingers tells me there's a moon,
but otherwise the morning waits.
Some crows are sleeping in the dead tree up the dune.
I see them shiver in the damp. Wars start like that
and horror movies.
Our laundry hangs forgotten on the line, the clothes still
soaked.
A spider made a web
between your dark-blue boxer shorts and the wooden table.
This is my world. I breathe in autumn air.
Old air, old earth, of moss and mould.
The crows awake, their screams are nails scratching a
chalkboard.
Above me lies the lid of leaden sky.
The day repeats itself and I am still amazed.

# Blue Forever

The sky over the trees says nothing in this blue,
no angels swim there, only birds but they are silent,
I might have hoped for something biblical to show
but there is only blue eternity and flocks of geese.
How can we think that gods live there? Why would they?

Maybe hell is blue; I can't see heaven in this pool of nothing
where clouds go when they float out of our sight,
dissolving, and stop existing over our heads.
They die and do so just like that. They are the big bang in
fast forward.
Even though a tree lives longer than a cloud, the gods
moved up into thin air.

I have seen faces, ships and castles fade this way.
I cannot understand the reason for this empty sky then.
Where does it start, how far is always and how far away
from me
should I be looking for a god? For a reason to think twice.
Where have they gone to? Out of the blue our myths began.

An angel comes to tell a virgin she'll be mother of God's son,
and where is Zeus hiding in the mean time? The sky is
always blue
behind the clouds. We have no business asking for a sign
I'm told.
A goose falls dead in front of me. Out of nowhere, from
above.
His feathers move in hauling wind, although the life is gone.

# Dance Trees

They wave at me from the other side of the window:
the trees, all dressed up for the big May event.
I want to join in the dance and rain pink blossom
but would it not look strange to the tulips
that already wonder why I allow dandelions to grow
next to their splendour. So I just wave back secretly.

# The Mother Buzzard

I met a buzzard on her way
to kill a mouse and feed her kin.
Against a blue sky, circling low,
detached from Earth, hunt to begin
she dived, and caught
and then let go.
But why? A buzzard doesn't care
about another creature's life.
I watched her fly without her prey,
it was her motherhood at test.
Her offspring cried for cruelty
but all stayed hungry in the nest.
She couldn't kill a mouse that day.

# Motherhood

She screams a sound
that goes through bones and rocks.
The gull is witnessing the drowning
of her wounded young.
Circling anxiously over the waves,
attempted rescue doomed to fail,
she cannot help. Her desperation
goes beyond what she knows safe.
She looks at me.

I hold the hands of both my young
that cry for what is going on.
Her fear of me forgotten, now she lands
before my feet. She waits till I take action.
I walk into the water for some steps,
but the undertow is quicker;
the young gull does not once emerge.

The mother flies,
stays above our heads awhile,
her screams are fading
in a hoarse cry over loss
before she sets off to the sea.
On the deserted beach, three crows
come looking for the small cadaver
when it's washed ashore.
I take my two back home
into the safety of the nest.
We hear her cry all day.

*Ina Schroders-Zeeders*

# Late Spring

When cold air is blowing
all the way from Siberia,
killing birds that should nestle
and a tulip that tries to rise from the soil,
like that, such bitter reward
is what we got from efforts
to be like others in our youth.

To be a tulip in frost.
To make a nest on frozen ground,
and find the little chicks frozen
and petals dead before bloom.
Spring comes late sometimes,
but then it bursts in thousands daffodils,
and with young birds singing all around.

# Frosted Air

What is the name
for the colour of frosted air,
I see it around the old barn
in the meadow.

It has no name, the shed,
no reason to be, it is
soon to be demolished
and frost will go away.

Spring is the answer to all.

# The Feelings of Flowers

Flowers have no feelings I assumed,
indifferent as they go with everything,
a funeral, a wedding, Valentine.

Some colours make the eye wonder
what nature can think of next.
No flowers ever objected to being painted
in absurd stripes or polka dots.

Yet I saw snowdrops shiver under snow
and daffodils mourn over their reflection.
When a rose loses its petals one by one, its pain
leaves a memory in the sweet scented air.

# Swans Know

Every swan knows this:
bow your head,
split the dark water
of the moonlit night,
as you approach her
silently in majestic beauty.

Fly away now and then
to spread your wings
but never leave her.

# Grey Sunday in February

After first glimpse this won't be a real day:
the weather is absent, people still sleep,
the calendar's stuck on yesterday's page,
the birds sit it out on rooftops and trees
where none of them move, and none of them sing.

Some little white flowers think it is spring,
they stand alone while the world's sleeping in.
If I wake you up to watch a grey day,
will it be better than sleeping so deep?
I'll give it a try. Watch the snowdrops with me.

# I Take the End of Winter Bad

The end of winter never felt more sad,
the geese that went, have not returned at all
and skies still have the greyish gloom of fall.
This year I take the end of winter bad.

I know that spring is only make believe
and life is not at all starting a new.
It gives me hope though to be so naïve
to think there can grow flowers out of slough.

I watch the days behind the window glass.
Life is on hold, maybe it won't return,
I cannot think that winter will soon pass
when every day I see prolonged sojourn.

The geese that went, have not returned since fall,
it's them I miss, their happy springtime call.

# Return

Sixteen geese, majestic in their flight,
knew by instinct that the time was right,
they left when frost started to freeze the land
and choose the best bird too be in command.

And so they left, excited as a team
to see places. Bright hearted they did seem,
I watched them with a frightened heart
and felt a sorrow when they did depart.

This morning from horizon, towards me,
five birds came flying home across the sea,
their feathers whispered right above my head
just five had made it, all the rest were dead.

In spite of loss, they did go on to tell
about their voyage, they came back from hell.

# Frosted Still

More the days grow longer each day,
the feeling there might be more to life
is coming back in bits by snowdrops.

But in the soil, the frost remains.
I am not about to sigh in relief.
There's a catch, no doubt.

# See This Tree

See this tree, this old tree,
branches torn off by the wind,
seasons tried to kill his spirit
but the leaves kept coming
and new branches kept growing
for so long, he never gave up.
My hope is a dying tree.

Watch this bird flying, circling
tired wings fighting the wind,
seasons tried to kill his spirit
but he kept on flying
and new birds flew with him
always, never giving up.
My hope is a flying bird.

# The Crow 2

The crow awaited here the end of day,
a black spot painted on the winter's sky,
as cold air took his horrid scream away.
The crow awaited here the end of day,
in quiet land where no one wants to stay,
his yell was echoing, 'twas time to die.
A black spot painted on the winter's sky,
as cold air took his horrid scream away.

And then it all was over for the prey;
the crow had killed, the prey was unaware,
in quiet land where no one wants to stay.
And then it all was over for the prey,
as cold air took its horrid scream away,
a frozen moment of a final scare.
The crow had killed—the prey was unaware—
in quiet land where no one wants to stay.

As night fell, I could hear the black crow cry,
as if regretting that he killed his prey,
he cried as if not wanting it to die.
As night fell, I could hear the black crow cry,
as if the crow was wondering why
his cruelty would never go away,
as if regretting that he killed his prey
he cried, as if not wanting it to die.

# 10 Beaufort

Expecting storm
I close all windows
close my eyes
and touch your hand,
expecting storm
along the shoreline,
the birds, some hide
but then some don't,
expecting storm,
the ships are safe now,
this will pass
once more, the tide
will try and win
but won't.
November storms
are always losers.

# Just a Bit of May

I go to sleep when all outside is light,
I rise and nothing changed, it's light out there.
Dreams come with no more darkness, no more night,
no signs of fear or none that I'm aware.

The blackbird sings before I go to sleep
and wakes me up each day at about five.
This time of year, this way, I'd like to keep
in mind as best of memories in life.

# Where It Was

And it was there,
right there
in the woods.

All I wanted to know,
it was in the light,
in the green of the leaves,
in the sound of the sea
at a distance,
all was there.

Birds sang in discussion,
I heard a cuckoo
and its echo
and the wind blew
with kind whispers,
explaining the world.

All was like it had been
forever
and all was there
for me to take in.

But I had to move on,
go home to watch
the six o'clock news
and I forgot
what it was
right there.

But it was all.
That much I know.
And it was there.

# The Trees

I walked through dunes in sunny spring
just passing trees I've always known.
I tried to climb them as a child,
I buried birds between their roots,
I brought my children here to play,
and birds made nests up in their tops.

My secret thoughts I shared with them
and here I stayed in hide and seek,
my tears were wept in their safe shade,
they sheltered me from rain and hurt,
their patient movements brought me rest
and I hoped that no tree was cut.

Their branches bended with our lives
as seasons came with frost and rain
and summer winds dried out their husks;
destroyed by fire, some of them.
When here the young man hanged himself
it was as if I heard them cry.

# Past Trees

I remember green meadows and
us, children playing in the grass,
how good it was,
who we have been
when trees were there for climbing.
We never fell.
We never felt further from then
than now we are grown up
and fallen is the tree,
the meadows gone forever.

# Indigo Night

while waiting for the night-bird's song
this indigo night we have snow
in snow you cannot wait too long
the night-bird might be frozen stiff
let's wait some more, if we don't go
there's always if, in deadly snow
we might find out it still does live

this indigo night we have snow
just walking in dreams with no sound
slender with grace the trees do bow
deep under the load that they bear
we know there is wildlife around
eyes lighten, move, not to be found
while hiding in holes everywhere

in snow you cannot wait too long
still the night-bird might be living
if all is well and nothing wrong
so we stand here and wait some more
for the music it'd be giving
all are waiting, all the living
like we waited in nights before

the night-bird might be frozen stiff
how will we know what happened here
so many creatures will not live
by dawn, they'll be deep frozen stills
a cry somewhere, of dead and fear
maybe a stray dog or a deer
or something that the night-bird kills

let's wait some more, if we don't go
we hear how the night-bird sings
and if it does, then we will know
that what we heard was more than life
it is one of the finest things
when in the snow a night-bird sings
and keeps it up till after five

there's always if, in deadly snow
what if we stay and never leave
why would we bother now to go
is it much better where we live
is there more hope or more belief
where all are hurting in their grief
while here the night bird wants to give

we might find out it still does live
the bird, the world, the hope for more
than what this winter had to give
if we just wait here in this cold
we have survived this way before
it is too far to the front door
so what we freeze and won't be old

# Under the Ice

Now death has come in white, covering all,
food and life, in a coating of plastic
sugar, not living continues, in, under, the ice.

As it must be cold there, where no one is,
the ice in the sea has no feelings for
those ships that have sunk in sight of safe ports.

But while slow frozen water is crushing
the coast, seagulls find a way to find fish
and the sun attempts to melt the cold earth.

# Birds of a Feather 2

As soon as it is light, I am walking in cold air,
dressed appropriately for the early hour of the day,
not for the cold though, of that I am well aware.

Off I go to feed the birds outdoors and see
them showing off in plastic colours green and blue
waiting with contempt for the softy likes of me.

One old blackbird, shy, grey, and picked at to the skin,
is watching me, approvingly for what I bring
shiv'ring in my pink thingy that is way too thin.

I also wear an old sweater someway next to grey
above green willies in a too big husband size
completing my outfit in a practical way.

The pretty birds rush off, high giggling from the sight
when humbly I put down the food for them to have,
so not the grey bird. She does stay and takes a bite.

So I am a killer for the hottest passion
but I do think that both the bird and I agree:
let them laugh as winter is no time for fashion.

# The Poetry of Birds

The birds are waiting for something to disturb them
and I oblige, I walk too close.
They fly up in beautiful disorder,
a poem each, and I watch the whole thing
until they land, united and silent,
watching me having hiccups, watching me
walking home slightly limping.

They won't feel the way I feel for them I think,
but who knows what a bird considers to be poetry.

# January Laziness

The afternoon drifted by us.
Calmly we sat,
both with our coffee,
no words needed
as we watched the clouds
and the winter birds pass.

Time to do nothing
but ponder how clouds
and birds come and go,
taking our thoughts
to go with them, from us,
forever and calmly away.
We drifted along with them
just for a bit
to see them off.

Then the phone rang
and the clouds moved on
into darkness.
But one wild goose
remained on a roof top
near a smoking chimney.

There is something to be said
for staying where it's warm
on a cold winter's day
and let others carry away
all weary thoughts.

*Ina Schroders-Zeeders*

# Anti-climax at Eleven

Evening calm is around us
A bird sings a song
So quiet we both are
Listen, a free concert

A bird sings a song
that no one ever heard
but is familiar to all
as it is about life

So quiet we both are
and no reason to talk
I cherish this silence
between us, and the bird

Listen, a free concert
that comes every evening
till the neighbour's cat
makes a move into the tree

# Their Branches Curving

No two trees are alike in their branches curving,
yet a tree is a tree for reasons of simplicity
and rows of trees can be seen as repeating plants.
Dig out a tree and plant it elsewhere, will it grow in
the same way? We can't tell. This one tree is unique
and how its branches whirl is not known until
the tree has ended its grow and is a tree in name.
But when is it fully grown?
We think we know, but we know nothing.
The unexpected is a tree, mocking all logic,
and no two trees will ever be the same.

# Morning Flirt

Upon the dune behind the town
I watch the sunshine finding ways
of moving me.

Every second, morning changes
in a rearranged embrace.

Beams through branches,
rooftops shining,
golden linings under clouds.

And no one here to share this,
I am alone and hold my breath
here, where such beauty lies.

If this is all for me, I have only
gratitude.

The day has started well.
The morning flirted with me.

# IV
## The Road to the Family Tree

# Watching from the Past

Sepia and faded the past is watching me,
eyes following my moves. The old portrait
tells me in every angle of the room
that I am not alone here as I dust.
Her eyes beg me to stay. I must.

How did she do that hair, I wonder, did she
shape it every morning in that way
or just on special days, like
when they had the photo made?
What was her life about? But she can't say.

For minutes she and I connect,
and for a moment I am her:
a woman anxious for the lens
as it may take her soul away.
I feel the blame—did I disturb her grief?

I smile and now her lips seem curved.
I leave the room to go on with my day
but she stays in my mind, ancestor with my name.

# Connection

Where my grandfather's father walked,
I walked the same way to the sea;
where his eyes saw clouds above him float,
so do I see them drift in changing shapes,
and though we never met,
I feel him close to me.

My footsteps here won't last a day,
before the wind blows sand all over,
but once there comes a child to see
these dunes, this water, and this sky
and, though we never met,
will then remember me.

# Grandfather 1

The moment of our last goodbye,
you almost lying in your coffin,
me too curious for questions,

so dark it was that evening,
one lamp burning where you lied,
the morgue in the old people's home.

Your eyes, still open, seemed surprised
that death had taken you. I left, but
kept the light on later in the night.

You never came to haunt me though.
My guess is that you felt all right
wherever they had made you go.

And sometimes when the day is grey
and all cries death, I share your view,
the last time that you took a breath.

# Becoming Mother

Days when inside you
a new person is growing,
are longer days, intensely;
more than before,
you are aware of life
and how fragile it is,
feeling its strength
in every fiber of your existence
as a bond is achieved
and now you know
how the chain is forged,
why you cry
over spoiled milk and daisies.
It has always been so
for mothers-to-be.

# Cold Start

The loud screaming baby, bundle of joy,
traumatized by former lives,
is carefully taken to the father
whose ears hurt more than
anesthetics can prevent.
He lies a smile in disbelief.

Life starts in flabbergasting cold.
A lonely journey begins
from the moment the womb is left.

Loud screaming starter in the hurdle race
of which the distance varies;
your finish appears vaguely on the horizon,
an uncertain blur trembling in hot air,
and although you are too fragile,
too small, too alone:
go for it.

You are a winner anyway for making the effort,
no matter if the wind's against you.
No matter if the race is short.

# Tall He Stood There

Tall he stood there,
he, my father,
me a toddler,
he a stranger.

Shadow caught him,
just a figure
out of nowhere
he appeared.

High he raised me,
he, my father,
on his shoulders
I was placed.

"He's your father,"
said my mother—
there, beneath us,
she seemed smaller.

Close the sky was,
gone the earth now.
He, my father,
he was home.

# Family

Having family
should be a vaulted passage
to a life ahead

# Warmth

There must have been a hole in the diaphragm
or you would not have been born,
and now you look at me, wondering if I shall feed you.
Yes I shall. My body wants to, so I suppose it is the thing
to do.
Your trust in me is encouraging.

Outside birds fly around with straw for their nests,
reminding me I have no place for us.
You had been better off being a bird,
but we shall do with our imperfect start together
and you are, you are, the most beautiful.

# Nose

Four photos gone from the light they were taken in,
the short parade that hardly forms your life, lying on the table now,
two of them made of you as a mobilized soldier,
a face with a long nose and frightened eyes
(this is just before you met my grandmother in Rotterdam),
none of your wedding in 1919,
one of you with a basket of bread,
and one of which no one knows is it really you.

All of them fading now,
and these lines will only be read
by those who never knew you nor heard you
while I remember best your trembling voice
singing in the old people's home
where we never took pictures.
The song was about a lord being your shepherd
and of lush meadows where you never wanted to be. Grass is for cows.

Your face serious and beautiful, paper white and pink,
will live on sepia forever in a closed photo-album.
I have no pictures of you and me together
though I knew you for fourteen years.
You left no inheritance, they say.
You even had to sell your wedding ring for food.
I do feel you are in my blood and more so in my face.
I've got your nose and I do like to sing when you are in my mood.

# Father's Hand

I do not remember your hand in mine
but you once lifted me on your shoulders
but you once hit me in the face
but your hand was the hand of a father
you were my father and I remember you well
but not your hand in mine ever

# Father 1

All the stuff he once saw
was raging through his veins
and he said he couldn't speak,
and his eyes tried to stay dry in water
as the forgotten war had broken his mind,
forever remembered through his pain.

He saw the slippery killers approaching
in the land where he had to fight,
where no one knew him. Where they hated him.
East Indies. He saw his friends die or get dark,
a darkness they would share in the light
of coming post war years.

When he came back, no one cared much for his pain.
The good people were gone, the others survived.
Everyone was trying to make the best
of what remained of humanity.

He sailed the world. He could not get away though.
He got a wife and child and did what he should do.
He never shed his tears but he
did show his anger. Life failed him and so did I.
He was a father with a history, but so had she,
all parents had such histories and trauma.

And the darkness approached us
in bright summer mornings.

Days were ruled by his wife, her past perhaps,
as cruelty came out to play her mind.
What would be next. Her moods would change.
I was never sure. Nor was he when he was home.
And with all that stuff that never left
his aching body, his thoughts,
he went numb. He could not live this way.

After he died,
the graveyard was silent as he was,
as if peace was there to be found,
but death is silent too.

A whisper came through the trees,
and now we hoped this was better. An ease.

Shadows follow us. My darkness is a silent one.
I cannot speak of it. Why should I.
We all have our own moments of horror.

I try to be as brave as possible. As a soldier
in a foreign land that hates me. Take care
of your mother he said as he left. I was four and failed.
She watches me think and stops her play.

I never shed tears still she knows
that the darkness has come over me
now the evening shadows found me.

She looks at me. Not two years old,
she knows and smiles. And I smile too.
One day I shall take her to the place
where the trees whisper and my parents lie,
to tell her about love. And that it doesn't matter
that shadows come; they always go as well.

For now she is about to sleep
and I have found a candle to give light.

# Grandfather 2

I remember I could hear you read,
downstairs, turning the pages
in the silent house, it came through
the cracks of the floorboards in my bedroom
that let in the light from your lamp.

The sound of paper rubbing,
or of a finger moving
from difficult word to word,
the crisp noise
when you would shake the newspaper
as to order what was most important:
the Kennedy murder, the building
of the Berlin wall, or the weather,
and it is how I remember you.

The evidence that you were there
was in the calm sound of your reading,
the whispering voice that spoke
of a world we both did not understand.

# The Blossom

Someone had died and it was summer.
The funeral black items danced white on my retina
in the overkill of light.

I tried to find your hand
when the grownups fell quiet
and the deceased was carried out of the house.
A black bird sang.

A woman tried to find comfort in your eyes.

You looked at the yellow blossom on the coffin
more intensely and with more love
than you looked at her, away from her face,
though she was crying and the blossom
stayed indifferent for kindness.

Later I realised you once were friends.
Why do we do the things we do,
and for whom are we to be so cruel?

# Time 2

Standing by windows watching seasons
I see my grandmother and my mother
in the dark behind the glass but it is me.

Autumn leaves and the green of May—
same trees, but nothing stays the same;
time has the last say on every subject.

When guests stay for dinner,
after a while their jokes become old,
they push over wine glasses.

Time, an unwanted guest, an idiot
who crawls in memories as if it is a hole,
makes a nest of reality and messes it up.

Behind the dark windows stands
always the Reaper, with the face of my mother.
I have become her. Time has taken me over.

# Like

My deceased grandfather talked to me,
sitting with his ankles crossed as always,
the way all his offspring sit, including me.
He sat in front of his house, as usual.
However, his voice, a bit hoarse,
made no sense. He shook his head.

Being dead makes communication difficult,
but then again I don't remember
any conversation I had with him
when he was alive, so I enjoyed his effort.
He raised his thumb, as in a Like.
Maybe the afterlife is Facebook based.

# So Like You

So like you to tell me,
long after your death,
where rabbits run,
how to find the true North,
what the best place is for shelter
from rain, that ghosts don't exist
and beauty cannot be defined.
All is there in the eye
of the beholder, like I see you
everywhere in splendorous light.
Now I know where you kept God hiding.
So like you to save the best for last.

# The Man Becomes My Father

He and his friends
hunted on rabbits;
the dead corpses hanging in the shed
not undone from their fur
were the yield of that night,
the success, the triumph.

But in the morning,
sunrise in the shed,
I could hear him go there
and in the haze of the day
I saw his hand, so fragile now,
stroking an animal
he never wanted to kill.

# Old Ships in Mist

Not many stories made it safely from the old days,
so much lies buried under the surface
of tired waves that cannot reveal any secrets.
Whole families went down, not much to say;
we don't know where they washed ashore, if so,
but names passed on from one ship to another.

Albertje was the name given to my mother,
her father's mother's name. Not many pictures
made it from those salt, moist quarters.
I have an album but no names. Faded faces stare
with fear and smirk at the photographer, in Copenhagen,
Antwerp, Riga. Saint Petersburg. Groningen. Albertje.
Which is hers?

They tell me something with their eyes,
of life in storm at sea, of places far away,
though they were always home, like snails
or turtles. Some ships sailed on, though not with them,
their stories gone forever for the heirs. Sometimes in mist
a ship appears that no one knows. I am convinced it's
theirs.

# Son

Once you have reached your truth, draw me a house
and tell me where the living is, your door,
what carpet there is on the wooden floor,
what is your house like, does it hold a storm?

Once you have settled for the man you are,
send me a postcard of the view from there,
show me the white clouds moving through your air,
let me believe that you have found it.

# Caught

Fishing means both of us crying,
me and my son who's only five,
both sad because the hook has pierced
the slimy cheek of the small sprat,
that looks with one eye where it lived
and one into my soul that dies,
it knows that all is lost. Sweet life.

My eyes half closed I free the fish
and feel the flesh reluctantly
let go of metal. Hope returns.
Son puts it back into the sea
where in surprise it swims away.
Blood on our hands we are relieved.
(Son held his breath accordantly.)
Another male is passing by;
Son waves the angle with bravour.

"We caught a fish!" And let it go,
but I won't tell. We buy some fish
and chips for home, no eyes are seen,
no questions asked. He takes my hand.
We let a sprat go well mature.

# The Child is Here

The child that gave you pain is me,
the troubles and the fights were me,
and on your grave I find no token
that you have forgiven me,

except for a breeze that comes from the sea,
a cloud in the shape of a smiling face,
a flower that grows on your silent grave,
but have you forgiven me? What token should there be?

I just see a raindrop that slides down as a tear
over the words that say "the beloved one,"
and there is a bird that sits on the stone
watching me spell the name that is you.

So the child that gave you pain is here,
looking on your grave to find a token
that says all the words we should have spoken.
The child is here. Maybe the father is here too.

# Last Time

Last time I talked with my grandmother
she was stage diving in her mind
from the podium into the hands
of her dead audience of Nazis,
Danish fishermen, and begging Polish children.

Nothing was as it seemed,
all was gone from normality
into a world of her own
and she thought I was someone
she didn't know. She called me Mrs.

Last time I had a talk with my mother
the same thing happened, so I can say
without being too pessimistic
there is a fair change I shall go bonkers as well.

# Old Man of Mine

Old man of mine, we shared a lot I know.
I hear your thoughts before they are well said,
and know your groaning, you don't mean it bad.
I know you well, you know me much more so.

Recycled wisdom, such we never found
in books, with all we needed in ourselves,
those books can stay there on the shelves.
We throw them from us on the ground,

where we made love and we still do, old man,
and so much still is a surprise in life.
I put my arm in yours. I am your wife.
We go together growing old. We can.

Old man of mine, I knew you young and now
I get you all and whole. Once I know how.

# Togetherness

Back together and all safe, for now,
we throw marshmallows through the air,
singing carols by the crooked tree,
this moment we are being family,
just for a moment all my offspring are here.

I can feel and touch their presence; see,
take in, to last me for another year.

What the future will be, no one knows for sure,
uncertain times are on the calendar,
I fear so much for each and every one,
sometimes I think that now our luck is gone,
as a darkest gate the new year waits right there,
how lighter days and happiness seem done
with us, what will there be for all, and where?

Back together and all safe for now,
what the future will be, no one knows for sure,
we throw marshmallows through the air.
Uncertain times are on the calendar,
singing carols by the crooked tree,
I fear so much for each and every one.
This moment we are being family.

Sometimes I think that now our luck is gone.
Just for a moment all my offspring are here,
as a darkest gate the new year waits right there,
I can feel and touch their presence; see
how lighter days and happiness seem done.

# Mothers

On rare occasions
such as birthday parties,
the mothers would smoke
filtered cigarettes
and it had to be done in the kitchen
where they giggled like teenagers.
They went to the hairdresser
to get curls once a month
and on birthdays, they used hairspray.

On other occasions
such as funerals in rain
and Tupperware parties
they would smile sadly,
lips painted red,
the curls covered with head cloths,
and when another baby was born
they would do both and cry hard, giving tea parties
using Tupperware containers for cookies
that would taste plastic.

I don't wear lipstick often
and I do not smoke.
I don't care too much
for birthday parties,
I don't own any Tupperware,
and I try to avoid going to funerals.
I liked having all my children
and I never have cookies
when they come by the house.

# I Would Not Fit in My Own Childhood as a Mother

But maybe they went out
to drink wine later in the day, and read
philosophical poetry
with total strangers,
not understanding anything
but falling in love
and waking up in a motel
next to a god.

Now I can relate to that.
Yes, I could be
a mother in the sixties. If I had to.
If you were that god and if
there was a Tupperware container
that I could actually open
to give cookies.
But only
if I was not my child.

I could not do that part.

# Mensch

The train was packed,
my mother and I
went back to our country,
after a few weeks
on board with my father.

The journey took several days by train.
We sat on green benches,
the last part of the journey with some Spanish men
who were eating olives all journey.

They offered us some, but we didn't like.
They drank wine and laughed much.
They had a lot of suitcases and bags.

We crossed a border once more,
and the train stopped.
Custom officers entered.
The Spanish men
got agitated, panicked.
Without knowing their language
my mother knew why.
They had no papers and needed to run.

They wanted to take
all their luggage, but there was no time.
"Go," my mother said.
To make herself understandable,
she used her hands.

"I will put the luggage
out through the window."
Did she have no respect for uniforms?
They left in a hurry
and my mother did as promised.

The train then left
a few moments later.
My mother seemed pleased
that she had been able
to help the poor Spanish men.

Then, the last thing we saw,
was how the customs officers
had caught up with them
on the platform.

They took the men away.
My mother cried for them,
feeling their defeat as her own pain,
as they were poor sods,
trying to earn a living.

She was a Mensch.

# Aunt

The tablecloth stains carefully covered
by means of a vase with plastic flowers,
an ashtray never used,
two framed photos of people she never cared for
and the dust-collecting bible:
she hides well and goes through her hours
in silence. She knows more of covering up
than her pale eyes reveal.

# Father 2

Waves come rolling, gulls are unaware of me.
This beach has everything to remember
and looking for you, I find you right there.

The colour of your eyes, that is the sea.
I feel no cold although it is.
And besides: I am your child. I don't go anywhere.

You lifted me in your strong arms one day,
that is the best part that will linger on,
the image of you as my father, then.

I hear the sea that tells me not to stay,
using your voice, although you are long gone
from when alive and still a healthy man.

I should move on and know the waves don't care
that I feel better when they treat me nice
instead of ordering me that I must go.

But I'm your child, I won't go anywhere
because the sea reminds me of your eyes
and I do miss your arms around me so.

# Floating Marigolds

My mother's family had always lived on water
sailing from port to port, working, eating, sleeping
between sea and sky, or giving birth
on a rocking vessel
in the scent of tar and salt.

They never had much knowledge of earth
but once living on land my mother grew marigolds.
She was happy with them
till drunken vandals took them out
and threw them in the harbour.

A man later told us he had seen the flowers
drifting off to sea. Little orange dots
that tried to keep floating.
Watching my mother cry, she and I both knew
some flowers never make it ashore.

# Kitschy Moments

When my mother lost her life,
many years before her death,
I could not cope well
and I cried in the garden,
as she did in the nursing home.
Never were we both so alone.
Then a butterfly landed on my hand,
I remember I thought it a kitschy moment.

It stayed there till my tears were over.
When I finally returned
to my mother, days later, she
who had never done any drawing,
drew what to me looked like a butterfly
on the steamed window.
She said it was a handkerchief
and I agreed. But it was a butterfly.

From then on, in other kitschy moments,
in leaps of time, in hidden meanings,
if I looked beyond, I found answers.
Now and then we understood
that words could move silently between us
like our thoughts. Her eyes spoke for her.
She had forgotten me,
but her body knew I was the child she carried.

*Ina Schroders-Zeeders*

# Aware

While we were holding hands
waiting for your death
I heard someone playing
the accordion in the hallway.

The new arrival in the home,
she used to live in our street,
she played sad and beautiful,
did you hear it too?

Like how 'twas played
when we lived next to the café,
every Saturday they did, so festive.

Well, you never liked music much.
I think you wouldn't have appreciated the moment.
But I did.

My last memory of you,
and there was music, Mama.
'Twas right there.

While the funeral started, the sun broke out
through the grey skies, and rays
of warm golden light shone over us.

We all carried a white rose each,
that would join you in the grave
and it was almost festive,
did you notice too?

Like how you'd loved
your winter birthdays to have been,
and so many people walked behind you.

Well, you never liked people much.
I think you wouldn't have appreciated the moment.
But I did.

My last memory of you,
and there were people, Mama.
Everywhere.

While your coffin slid into the grave, I felt
how you were glad the whole
thing was over so now you could rest.

The silence you needed, came then
with the rest you well deserved
and it was almost serene,
did you shiver then too?

Like how your life
should really have been, much more so.
And we were at peace together for once.

Well, I think you would have liked that.
And we both would have appreciated each other so.
But I did.

My last memory of you,
and there was loving, Mama.
I'm aware.

# Your Face, Your Voice

I saw a face in setting sun
that I adored, a face so old
in quietness, but young in looks.
I heard a voice in evening prayer
that I found dear, a voice so young
in timelessness, but old in words.
It was your face, it was your voice,
Papa. I dreamt of you last night.

# Needed

Saturday afternoon, a minute to five,
the seafaring son called to mention
that he was on his way to the ferry,
as he would be home for a while.

Through the storm and hail
his father and I hurried
to the store for food and such,
and although complaining,
we couldn't hide a smile.

We are Mum and Dad once more.
We will feed the son, we'll listen
to his stories (without grasping much)
and though we know it will be just for now
it feels good to be, a little, needed.

# Older

Now I see the child I carried,
how he ages, becomes father,
and time never went so fast
as when I shrank some inches
beneath his shoulder, fading
on my way back to where I was before.

# The Call

Not sure how this day will end she stands
giving water to the plants
that might survive the winter.

Her grandchild will be born today.
Though quiet is the room,
the clock is ticking louder now.

Geraniums are still in bloom.
The waiting occupies her mind,
making coffee keeps her busy.

A grandchild will be born today,
the coffee's getting cold,
the clock ticks louder
so she covers both her ears.

And then there is that call.
She takes a breath of air,
a prayer of some sort is said
before she answers. "Yes?"

# Teaching Eline How to Walk

You're seven months, holding my hand
and there it is, you feel the earth
beneath your feet, oh dear, you stand.

Your eyes check mine, is this okay?
You swiftly smile, before a boom,
the moment gone, oh dear, you land.

# Never Be Before

What is strange about this picture
of you, my little granddaughter,
is that your smile,
that finally showed up,
after a sobbing while,
has made me cry.

By now you aged some hours more.
Already you will never be "before."
Life doesn't really have a *why*.

# Chain

The bracelet belonged to my mother's grandmother,
my grandmother's mother, my great-grandmother,
my granddaughter's great-great-great-grandmother,
and it was made of the chain of a watch
that belonged to god knows whom.

And one day it will be hers,
my granddaughter's, to pass it on
to her granddaughter, and she will say:
"This once belonged to your great-great-great-great-great-
grandmother,
my great-great-great-grandmother,
your great-great-grandmother's great-grandmother,
the mother of your great-great-great-great-grandmother,"
and the kid won't give a damn.

# Shadows

I am lonely in the middle of offspring
and think how lonely others are.
And days go on with no reason.

I live because I breathe.
Almost evening now.
The grandchild plays.

She makes the most of her hours
while I sit and watch
shadows approaching.

So alone. But I breathe on.
I do that much.
There is the face of my father in hers.

# Why Mothers Cry

There is no word yet to describe the loss
that I felt, each time, after giving birth,
when the empty womb was useless and abandoned,
as all should be about the joy that is new born.
Many words are said about child birth
but silenced, underneath the stretched out skin,
there was safety.

I was all around you to protect you
and to fight for you with my own flesh
and my own strength. Yet there is no word
to describe my tears for you,
once you were on your own. What had I done,
I made you enter a cruel world that has no name
to call the dearest kind of love.

*Ina Schroders-Zeeders*

# On the Bus

My granddaughter takes the bus with me,
probably her first time.
She is too short to look out
the window but she doesn't want to
sit on my lap, she is content
just watching a photo
of the bus that is hanging
in the bus
and the fact that we are there,
in that bus, means
we are also in that photo.
She claims she can see us
and she waves. I see us too.
We drive on and get to know
the essence of travel: to be there
watching ourselves in a bus in a bus.

# Rejection

My toes love the sand.
The first little wave
to find the beach
draws back when we touch.

Mothers lift little naked children
when the waves get higher
but they cry,
they want to feel the sea.

We sleep naked under a sheet
that moves by the welcome draught.
Skin, we are all skin in summer.
I watch the beige of your back
where the shape becomes half a moon
and lighter. We sleep together
in a bed too large to find us back.

When we are born,
the first thing they do to us
is clothing,
to put distance between the child,
its dirt, and the mother.

When we are dead, even then,
we are dressed up.
My mother is buried in a nylon dress,
her favorite, because
dirt fell off it and she liked clean.

Long after her bones are gone,
her dress will be there,
unchanged by time, untouched by earth.

I want to be naked
when I am put in a hole in the sand,
somewhere near the shore.
Maybe the sea will want me then
and not reject me.

# Generations

One night my father
who came home from sea
took me in his arms outside
to watch the stars
sticking on the cobalt sky
and all I saw was him.

I held my son just after
he began to live and
said goodbye to us as one.
From then on he was someone else,
and were we strangers
passing by.

For centuries grandmothers
have managed to live
in the presence of baby
granddaughters
so I can bear your crying.
I am your granny. Give in.

# V
## The Road to the Sea

# The Sea Is My Mother

With waves her arms the sea is my mother,
she rocks me slowly when I am a child.
When I disobey her, her senses go wild
and she keeps me away from the world.

When I love, my mother approaches
on the beach she observes and approves.
When we hug, she reclines in her moves
to leave us alone during neap tide and ebb.

With my children about to be born,
she hugged me tender and whispered a name.
Every time as I called her, she came
giving strength in the rhythm she rocked me.

When I die I shall walk through the waves
finding arms that forever will hold me
as my mother is always the sea
always there to look after me well.

# Mist

Doubt sneaks up
slowly, a mist
between you and me
on a deserted beach.
I'm blinking twice;
you are gone
perhaps
or not.

# Forgotten Vision

A clear day made me see beyond blue,
water reflected a deepest sky.
I could see forever through and through.
There I rested and felt calmer too,
like so often with the sea nearby.

Without a search I found something there,
my mind was rinsed of bother and pain.
The silent sea and the soothing air,
an inner strength I had not been aware,
gave me the power to restrain.

The water wrinkled as thoughts returned,
it shivered, a cloud hung over me.
The vision went, not sure what I discerned
nor what the lesson was I learnt
I walked away, and let it be.

But years from then my memory knew
as I stood on the quay to watch the sea.
The vision came back, I saw what to do
to let go of my thoughts. The northern wind blew
and brought the clearness back to me.

# The Place

Not far from my home is a place
I come every time when I walk;
a space just to see nothing changed.

Ships go by and the ferry leaves port;
people wave. The sea wears the colour
of lead or is blue. Sometimes green.

Seagulls decide not to be fed
by passengers throwing pieces of bread,
enough to feed all. The birds are not keen.

They stay circling over my head,
maybe just for a talk as they
might be messengers and you sent them off.

If I listen with care I may know
what it is that you're trying to say,
why it was that you had to go.

# My View

From where I stand the world is sea,
this isle a boat that doesn't move,
and now and then some seagulls come
to tell us of how life goes on
over the edge that splits
the water from the sky.
Their mournful screams keep us in place.
From where I stand the sea is world,
I'm on a boat that is an island.

At times when air is clear
I watch a bit of world across the water:
some windmills show, churches emerging
all pale and trembling, not sure of their shape.
From where I stand the world looks an illusion,
where birds escape from every now and then
to tell us that it is not better elsewhere either.
From where I stand I know the world is sea,
but from your point of view this merely is an island.

# Sea Dance

You sometimes take more space inside my mind,
then roll away to where I cannot find,
as if you are an ocean of some kind.

Where does the sea begin, where does she end?
The waves are always moving towards sand
in an eternal dance of sea and land.

# The Book

A book is lying
on a bench in the park
and the pages are turned
by the wind.

The words are fading
and they drown in the rain
as the poem is washed
down the sewer.

A silence comes down
for a while all is lost
then the water finds way
to the sea.

A difference is made
on a shore, when a wave
comes on land and a gull
calls out loud.

A book is lying
on a shore, on a beach
and we think it was brought
by the wind.

# The Tide Turning

When the tide was almost turning, waves paused,
all seemed on hold. The clouds stopped moving on,
and we had time to find out what had caused
the gap between us, as so much had gone.
We stood there, not in water, not on land;
a seagull awaited our decision.

There was no sound, no movement on the strand.
What were we both trying to envision?
Then there it was: this lightning struck above.
The waves began to move up on the beach,
our feet got wet, and from thereof
we had each other: maybe this was love.

# Standing on a Dune

We are both watching the sun set.
I don't know you; you don't know me.
I see you wipe a tear.

It was a great sunset.

# Grain

Like a grain of sand in the wind,
when a storm blows over land,
losing touch, flying your way
across waves before landing
in cold water, sinking into sea
to be forgotten,
this is my love for you.

It won't reach you in due time
but like the grain it will stay put,
remain and waiting without change
as part of this earth
amongst so many others
that wash back to the shore
to become a piece of strand again.

My love for you won't leave me
even in this storm. Like a grain
it is solid, indestructible.
It might sink into sea, but will return.
Like a grain of sand on the beach,
it has a chance that you will find it.
And that your hand will lift it up again.

# On the Beach

Fading shadows mean you are forgotten by the sun, my friend,
your footsteps blown away by a north-western storm,
the seagull cries above your absence, overrules your faint goodbye
that might have lingered on a calmer day,
only what you said before remains between us
to live on awhile before that too is gone.
This beach is now deserted.

New clouds, new dangers may take over.
New shadows chase me over land. I stand alone here on this isle,
searching for our truth in the seabird's silent stare
and for a moment I do see you, a reflection in its eye:
you turn away from me. Yes, we are through
and will be strangers from now on.
I know and watch the seabird fly over the greyish waves.
The end.

# Shadow

A lonesome figure near the shoreline,
your shadow drifted over the water
after your last words were gone,
after the tide washed the beach
rinsing memories we had to let go of.

Nothing remains to hold on to,
hear, silence falls over the waves
and water slips through my fingers.
Now and then the sea whispers
of days we could have been together.

I see your silhouette every time
I am there. I feel your presence,
as if you are walking beside me
but none of it is real now. Those days
are shadows moving fast away from land.

# Worth the Walk

What did I try to find:
the beach was wet and empty sand,
maybe a bottle washed ashore,
a note perhaps inside,
or a feather, shells,
the footsteps of a child?

I did not find any of those.
Today I found a thought
that got me through the day,
unsought, it came in with the tide,
a treasure I could not hold in my hand,
it was a notion that this life was good.

# Possibilities

Seas, sheets of white paper, roads:
all meant for possibilities to happen.
I watch the sailing ship go north,
the voyage of the brave,
and seagulls follow them
trusting that fish will emerge.

What possibly could go wrong:
a calm, a storm, or mutiny,
all calculated and accounted for.
Yet the story can take any turn,
as you might find
the road back home to me
or not.

# Rain on a Dune

I'm standing in amazement under skies
and watch the clouds fly faster now than birds,
they all seem on the run. I stay and wait
to witness what it is they're fleeing from.

Ships sail away and all is leaving me.
One person on a dune I feel too small
to understand. The rain is pouring, now
above me all is grey. The birds are gone.

But when I'm drenched, my feel of losing
at its worst, the grey breaks in a sudden crack
to leak a beam of sunlight over water.
Some birds come back. One ship returns, full sail.

# Waiting for the Tide to Kill Me

The beach is more a desert now,
the sea has run away somehow;
to drown myself the waters lack
in empathy, they won't allow.

If I wait long, the sea comes back
(if not belated by some wreck),
whom can I trust to help me go?
My footsteps are a desperate track.

The table of the tides I know
by heart but sea deceits me so,
there's only sand and shells to see.
I shall not feel defeated though.

Six hours I shall wait and be
the patient suicidal me
and then the water does the deed
and I am swept off both my feet.

# Homesick of the Sea

The sand is blowing under sky.
Can one be homesick of the sea?
I feel the grains inside my lungs
and every ancestor with me
is holding hands behind my back.

I feel their old eyes in my neck.
We walk the tide line just once more.
I never felt land was my home,
I am not meant to be ashore.
The waves as always seem to call.

The ancestors have seen it all
and tell me it is better so
to live on land and not at sea.
My guess is that it's what they know,
they've witnessed so much in their lives.

The sailing men, their sailing wives,
the storms they knew when all seemed lost,
the bitter struggle to maintain,
to be at sea at such high cost.
I walk back home leaving the waves.

# Murmuration

The murmuration shaped itself into a giant bird,
and swiftly moved as one, a joyful flirt with sea and sky,
I don't know why they did so for my very eyes.

They did it with no wings colliding, their unity
made me feel humble as a human, as far
away from murmuration seemed humanity to me.

# Wrecked

In early morning, by the raging sea,
where many ships were wrecked to pay
for greed, it gives an eerie feel
to think how once their men have seen this sight:
the sand that blows across the waves and shore,
and shells spread further than my eyes can find.

The men had seen such waves and knew the kind,
and wondered where their safe harbour could be,
then realized they would come home no more
as all was lost to them in every way.
Their dreams would stay afloat, while distant light
was luring them to sands under the keel.

# The Last Thing

Once
the sea was full with dying men
drowning in storms
never washed ashore,
but the last thing they saw
was a woman combing her hair.
It was seaweed,
but men
are like that.

# Ambergris

Now and then when the sea was more at ease
we walked looking for shells and bottles carrying notes
across the beach, the sand under our feet
but colourful plastic and fisherman's nets
were treasures we took home, and wood,
a stone that was said to be vomit of whale.
So rich is the sea. We kept the rotting wood and not the vomit.
What did we know of ambergris, we just knew about puke.

# Sea

I stood before a tempest sea once more,
she should be older then but seemed the same,
her waves rolled near my feet as times before
and loud she called me by my proper name.

She smiled at me when rays of sunlight shone,
her comfort whispers told me I should stay
in life to do what needed to be done,
she often told me I should go my way.

I could not join her, swim away and go
and leave all matters that I want to part
with every movement of the undertow
away from shore into a wanted start.

Sea would not have my company that day,
withdrew in low tide and in silent grey.

# Lost

Can I borrow
a bit of smile,
a shoulder,
someone's whispers
that all will be fine,
so I feel safer on this Baltic sea,
with waves in dark green shades,
yet sunlight on water?

And maybe I need to steal
some of a bedtime story-trust,
for a happy ending
on our white sailing ship
finding its way
back to the port
of Hamina.

Can I have some childish faith
that this journey
will bring us to port?
Even now
the ship is sinking, the
captain's drunk
and the compass lost.

# Alone I Walk

alone I walk over a silent beach
where once we played as children
our footprints are no longer here
but I keep looking for them still
each of our childhood days I find
in sand and salty memories in time

# Moment of Silence

Only whispers of the breeze
we hear, a sea that is resting now,
and we feel the first light
from the sun after the storm
touching our skins.
I am grateful to capture
this moment
of silence
for us.

# Misty Morning in November

The golden rays of autumn now are gone,
mist hangs around as if forever
and ships get lost at sea quite easily.

I hear the fog horn sadly cry all day.
Mist hangs around as if forever,
a blanket covering all of me,
hiding meanings still unspoken.

And ships get lost at sea quite easily;
if not guided by that weary sound,
they might get stranded on a bank.

I hear the fog horn sadly cry all day
luring sailors to our port for shelter,
like your words want peace with me.

# Best of Mornings

I was woken by a whispering sea,
the wind had turned and now was West,
the window open, a breeze was telling me
words, never spoken, a fairytale
so beautiful I closed my eyes
and dreamt again, quite heavenly.
The day had started with a feel of nice.

# Best of Gifts

A feather washed ashore and stayed on land,
remaining a reminder of a flight gone wrong.
Above the waves some murmurations end
before they reach a place to sing their song.

A shell is waiting to be seen, a hand
will pick it up, a treasure found among
debris. So much the sea gives to the strand;
this shell, though, has been dead for very long.

From where I watch the waves foam on demand,
no life seems present, yet the sea moves on,
the clouds mourn on this funeral event,
the smell of salt decay is very strong.

So all seems dead that comes ashore from sea,
but still it makes the best of gifts to me.

# Learning to Live

Desire to live on in spite
comes from walking near the sea,
from that overwhelming scent
of seaweed, tar, and salt,
and from the movement of the waves.
Sea is the womb
where good thoughts grow.

So many lives and deaths
already passed this shore,
new starts always emerged
out of the deep dark nothing.
Giving up is easy, the sea indifferent;
to beat the undertow
means more to me perhaps.

I want to see the beige clouds
before rain, the grey skies after,
and remain in spite of all.
A proper sea will challenge every beach,
will never give up trying
to leave some proof of her attempts.

# Devastated

When she, in storm and spring-tide,
stretches her arms,
empties her guts,
alters the beach
in a sizzling cruel crescendo;

when she vomits, foams,
wreaking destruction over land,
pouring her salty tears,
it's then I do love her the most:

sea, demented granny, not yet amortized, fighting,
holding on to life,
tearing up all she encounters,
spitting ensis, throwing crab onto the sand,
she shows her dirty teeth
(the driftwood that is splintering)

and crying whales are washed onto the shallows.
She fights her demons like a lioness.

Then wind clams up and all falls silent, she nourishes her wounds
and quietly returns to far and silent grounds.

# Washed Ashore

I have found so many treasures:
a bottle with a note on higher ground,
three books the sea has read but spit right out,
remains of an old sailor's bed,
and coins, a small amount, a bomb.

Where do they come from,
I don't know. At lower tide
the sea always surprises me
with objects and with thoughts,
with sounds and light,
and footsteps going nowhere.

# Acknowledgments

A very special thank you to the inspiration for my writings in English, David Agnew. He is a retired psychiatry nurse, a talented writer and artist, and a dear friend.

Follow his blog: belfastdavid.wordpress.com

# About the Author

Ina Schroders-Zeeders was born in the Netherlands, on the beautiful tourist-destination island of Terschelling. Her fascination with the sea began at an early age as she and her mother would frequently accompany her Merchant-Marine-Captain father on his adventures. Ina has spent her whole life enjoying books of all kinds, staying involved with libraries and book sales, until finally becoming a novelist in the late nineties.

www.ingramcontent.com/pod-product-compliance
Lightning Source LLC
LaVergne TN
LVHW041247080426
835510LV00009B/620